On William Faulkner

Eudora Welty
On William Faulkner

UNIVERSITY PRESS OF MISSISSIPPI

www.upress.state.ms.us

The University Press of Mississippi is a member
of the Association of American University Presses.

Frontis: Collage by John Langston. Photograph of Faulkner from the collection of Dean
Faulkner Wells, photograph of Eudora Welty by Kay Bell

Library of Congress Cataloging-in-Publication Data
Welty, Eudora, 1909–2001
On William Faulkner / Eudora Welty.
p. cm.
Includes bibliographical references.
ISBN 1-57806-570-4 (cloth: alk. paper)—ISBN 1-57806-571-2 (limited: alk. paper)
1. Faulkner, William, 1897–1962—Criticism and interpretation. 2. Mississippi—In litera-
ture. I. Title: Eudora Welty on William Faulkner. II. Title.
PS3511.A86Z985614 2003
812'.54—dc21

2003007718

British Library Cataloging-in-Publication Data available

ACKNOWLEDGMENTS

For their generous assistance the publisher is grateful to Patti Carr Black, Lucius Lampton, M.D., Louis J. Lyell, Suzanne Marrs, Noel Polk, Elizabeth Welty Thompson, and Mary Alice Welty White.

The following text is copyrighted and used by permission of the Estate of Eudora Welty: "Review of *Intruder in the Dust*," "Letter in Defense of Faulkner," "Presentation Speech: The Gold Medal for Fiction," "Memorial Tribute: Author Gave Life to Fictional County," "On Faulknerian Time," "Review of *Selected Letters of William Faulkner*," "Speech in Celebration of the William Faulkner Postal Stamp."

The following text is used by permission of the respective copyright holders: "Postcard from Hollywood" © Estate of William Faulkner; "Meeting Faulkner" © the Estate of Eudora Welty and Special Collections Department, University of Colorado at Boulder Libraries; " Faulkner's 'The Bear,'" from *The Eye of the Story* by Eudora Welty, © 1978 by Eudora Welty, used by permission of Random House, Inc.; "Keynote Speech: Southern Literary Festival" © Eudora Welty, LLC, Eudora Welty Collection, Mississippi Department of Archives and History; "Welty on Faulkner © Hunter Cole; "Welty and Faulkner and the Southern Literary Tradition" © Noel Polk.

Illustration credits: William Faulkner portrait, collection of Dean Faulkner Wells; Eudora Welty portrait by Kay Bell, University Press of Mississippi, courtesy of Eudora Welty; caricature of William Faulkner, courtesy of the Estate of Eudora Welty; Faulkner in his sailboat, the *Ring Dove*, photo by Phil Mullen, collection of Dean Faulkner Wells; William Faulkner and Eudora Welty with the Gold Medal for Fiction, courtesy of David Stekert, Budd Studio; Eudora Welty with two likenesses of William Faulkner, collection of Hunter Cole; Eudora Welty with Jill Faulkner Summers, courtesy of the University of Mississippi, Public Relations.

CONTENTS

7

FOREWORD: WELTY ON FAULKNER

William Faulkner, a man of small physical stature but large literary worth, cast a long shadow in every direction. It spread not only over the writers of his native Mississippi and the South but also into the many corners of literary America and abroad. A private man, he resided in Oxford, more than 150 miles distant from Eudora Welty in Jackson. Being in the same state with the phenomenal Faulkner, Welty said, was like living near a big mountain.

The history of American literature continues to show that the fiction of Eudora Welty and of William Faulkner rose to the top. Indeed in the American South, a region Welty called "the cradle of storytellers," these two writers are ranked at the summit.

Yet Welty faced up to a hard fact.

"As a writer," she said to a friend in private, "I can never be better than second best in my home state of Mississippi." In a speech given in public, she declared Faulkner to be "our greatest writer."

No matter how fervently she wrote, she was reconciled to living in the juggernaut's path and in the shadow of the great rock. For Welty, however, writing was not a competition. She felt that each writer should do his or her very best. That was enough.

Although she cherished and honored her writing gift and never doubted or undervalued the worth of her own art, she acquiesced to the probability that she would not surpass the achievement of William Faulkner. Yet for her

9

William Faulkner and Eudora Welty

intellect, her artistic power, and her mastery of language and of any genre she attempted, she continues to gain ever-increasing appreciation. One day she may be ranked as Faulkner's peer or be proved wrong in her self-assessment. She may be perceived like Chekhov in the presence of Tolstoy or like a deep lake beside the big mountain.

Faulkner and Welty's homeland afforded space for more than one writer. Welty surmised this truth at the age of twenty-two while she was enrolled for graduate study at Columbia University. She did not miss the impact of Faulkner's notorious novel *Sanctuary*, published in that year, 1931. Although her state was demeaned in the national ken as a hotbed of throwbacks, she was secretly wanting to be one of its writers, reasoning that if Faulkner of Oxford could write novels and stories, she herself could harbor hope that two writers might emerge from hard-bitten Mississippi.

As the punishing blow of the Depression struck, she went home to Jackson and began to write stories. In Mississippi she witnessed the reality that sparked Faulkner's fiction and her own. By 1936 she became a published writer herself.

After her second book, *The Robber Bridegroom* (1942), appeared, Faulkner took notice of her. Wishing to lend encouragement, he typed a postcard to her from Hollywood. Her book, which he recently had read, continued to hang in his mind. Although he did not know Welty and although his impromptu, garbled note seems to confuse her work with Zora Neale Hurston's, he let her know he was standing by to give help.

She never called on him, never needed to seek his assistance. But throughout Welty's long career, her many obliging writings about Faulkner's work show that she gained from him, not directly by editorial guidance or influence but by the example of his fiction. Repeatedly she acknowledged Faulkner's commanding presence, joking that she was a "Yoknapatawpha-natic."

"Better than the rest of Southern writing," she wrote, "Faulkner's creation of Yoknapatawpha County stands for what I take to be a truth, that deeper than people, farther back than known history, is the Place."

She classified Faulkner's "The Bear" as "an apocalyptic story of the end of the wilderness," "the whole history of Mississippi."

"Spotted Horses," one of her Faulkner favorites, she praised as "an enormous, complicated story, weaving in all those strands of what's comic, and not for its own sake but as a means of enlightenment, of showing what's happening, of the pathetic and the extremely realistic, all meticulously observed. It's something that only Faulkner could have done."

The Oxford Eagle, the county newspaper published in Faulkner's hometown, captured a special comic spirit that Welty relished in Faulkner's books. After coming home from New York, she was hired as a Mississippi publicist for the Works Progress Administration. In the office she delighted in reading the unintended hilarity in the local news reported in county papers. But, for Welty, *The Oxford Eagle* surpassed all others. She was so taken by its deliciously provincial reports from Faulkner Country that on November 9, 1936, she wrote the editor and became a subscriber. Three days later her letter was printed on the front page:

I enclose one dollar, for which please send me at the above address The Oxford Eagle for six months. At the end of that time I'll try to find another dollar for the rest of the year. I have been reading your paper in our office (WPA publicity dept.) and wish to say that in county news I think you are without peer in any state; the flavor is all there. I think it so worthy of preserving that I have a scrapbook of your county news in my collection of Mississippiana. Please never discontinue your correspondence.

As she told an interviewer in 1972,

I used to take a lot of the state newspapers and in the old days I loved to read the Oxford Eagle. There was one woman whose name kept turning up there, but I always felt any name around Oxford was automatically the property of Mr. Faulkner. He had such perfect names. I don't know if this is true, but somebody once told me they mentioned a name to Mr. Faulkner and he said, "Yes, I know the name well. Can hardly wait for her to die" so he could use it.

It amused her to recount another apocryphal anecdote about how a pestering woman sent Faulkner a piece of original fiction for him to critique, a love scene. Impatient over getting no reply, she telephoned him to ask what he thought of her writing. "It's not the way I would have written it," Eudora quoted him, "but, honey, you go right ahead."

Some five years after receiving the postcard from Hollywood, Welty was a visitor in Oxford, and the modest Welty met the tightlipped Faulkner on his home turf. They dined together at a genial gathering of friends they had in common. This was their official introduction.

Beside Faulkner, Welty seemed self-consciously tall.

"He was a small man, wasn't he, Eudora?" a friend asked her.

"Yes," she quipped, "he came just about up to my vaccination."

Silent and shy, Faulkner stood mostly alone against the wall, smoking cigarettes.

"I never dreamed I'd meet him," she told an interviewer. She found him "humorous and gentle and quiet. He didn't say much. He liked a funny tale." After the meal, he relaxed, and everyone assembled around the piano and sang old hymns.

Faulkner evidently liked her, for he invited Welty and her friend John Robinson over to nearby Sardis Lake to sail with him on his boat, the *Ring Dove*. "I was so happy he invited me. I had a little trouble getting in the boat. It was out a little from the shore, and I was so shy I couldn't say, 'You mean get wet?' Anyway, that's what I did. Just waded out in the mud through the stobs and stumps, got in the boat, and he took me sailing. I don't think either of us spoke. That's all right. It was kind of magical to me. I was in the presence."

In this memorable encounter of two Mississippi greats, literature was never mentioned.

"I certainly wasn't going to bring it up," Welty said.

Nor did they become fast friends. Rather, they were acquaintances with respect for each other. In the thirteen years that passed after their meeting, Faulkner remained taciturn, but Welty continued to praise him.

Shortly before he died, it was literature that drew them back together. In 1962 the National Institute of Arts and Letters named him as the recipient of the Gold Medal for Fiction for his lifetime achievement. At the annual meeting in New York City, his fellow writer from Mississippi was designated to make the presentation. Performing a typically gracious, deferential act that acknowledged him as master, she quietly slipped the medal to him before going to the stage. For the public ceremony she read her prepared remarks and then handed him only the empty case. The prize already was in his pocket.

This book collects Welty's writings on Faulkner and concludes with a magisterial afterword by one of the most notable critics of Welty and Faulkner. It shows that time after time Welty returned to Faulkner's writings. The sense of place in his fiction was unerring in its natural and artistic truth, and it validated her own. The frequency with which she celebrates his work signals the evidence that William Faulkner was one of her touchstones.

Welty's comments on Faulkner reflect her modesty before the man and his books, her eagerness to praise him, her love of the country humor and folklore in his fiction, and her astounded wonder over the Faulknerian power to depict comedy and tragedy. Whether acclaiming him in her critical essays or shaming Edmund Wilson in a letter to the *New Yorker* for his undervaluing Faulkner in a review of *Intruder in the Dust*, Welty is ever Faulkner's apologist, admirer, and defender.

Without needing a champion, Faulkner gained one.

—Hunter Cole

CITATIONS

"Better than the rest of Southern writing"

"From Where I Live," *Delta Review*, November–December 1969, p. 69.

"'The Bear' . . . an 'apocalyptic story of the end'"

"The Short Story," in *Three Papers on Fiction* (Northampton, Mass.: Smith College, 1962), p. 44.

"'Spotted Horses' . . . an enormous, complicated story"

"On Camera: Welty on Faulkner," *Major Notes* (Millsaps College), VI (Spring 1965), p. 25.

"I used to take a lot of the state newspapers"

Henry Mitchell, "Eudora Welty: Rose-Gardener, Realist, Storyteller of the South," *Washington Post*, August 13, 1972, p. L4.

"I never dreamed I'd meet him" / *"I was so happy he invited me"*

Nicholas Dawidoff, "Only the Typewriter Is Silent," *New York Times*, August 10, 1995, p. C10.

On William Faulkner

Wm Faulkner

Caricature of William Faulkner
[1930s]

In addition to writing stories and taking photographs, Eudora Welty enjoyed drawing caricatures that she shared with a few close friends. During the 1930s she sent a series of these to Frank Hallam Lyell. Those he received included Welty's satirical views of the Sheik of Araby, Dracula, King Solomon, and several notables of the day—the Prince of Wales, Guy Lombardo, Dorothy Dix, Elsa Maxwell, Eleanor Roosevelt, Mae West, and William Faulkner. In the decade that she drew Faulkner's caricature, he was both lionized and vilified by the public. His fiction and his reputation were well known to Welty, for she had read his novels and stories as they appeared. He was featured on the front cover of Time *magazine (January 23, 1939), and his novel* Sanctuary *(1931), which scandalized delicate readers, was adapted by Hollywood as* The Story of Temple Drake *(1933).*

Postcard from Hollywood
[1943]

In 1943 Eudora Welty was surprised to receive this impromptu praise from William Faulkner, who was living in Hollywood. The Gilded Six Bits *is by Zora Neale Hurston. Djuna Barnes is the author of* Nightshade. *"Green" is in the title of Welty's first book,* A Curtain of Green and Other Stories, *published in 1941. Welty's* The Robber Bridegroom *was published in 1942. There is no record of any reply Welty may have sent in response to Faulkner's offer of assistance or to his request for biographical information.*

27 April.

Dear Welty:

You are doing fine. You are doing all right. I read THE GILDED SIX BITS, a friend loaned me THE ROBBER BRIDEGROOM, I have just bought the collection named GREEN somthing, haven't read it yet, expect nothing from it because I expect from you. You are doing very fine. Is there any way that I can help you? How old are you?

When I read THE ROBBER BRIDEGROOM I thought of course of Djuna Barnes, the same as you thought of Djuna Barnes. I expect you to pass that, though.

Do you mind telling me about your background? My address is below, until July.

William Faulkner
% Warner Bros. Studio,
Burbank, Calif.

Meeting Faulkner
[1949]

*During the spring of 1949, Metro-Goldwyn-Mayer was completing the filming of
William Faulkner's novel* Intruder in the Dust *in his hometown. The excited citizens
of Oxford awaited the movie's world premiere at a local theater in October. Near the end
of August and amid the fervor Eudora Welty and John Robinson, a friend to whom she
had dedicated two of her works ("The Wide Net" and* Delta Wedding*), arrived for a
visit with his friend Nancy Farley.*

*During this weekend in Oxford, Welty and Faulkner met two times. They were intro-
duced to each other at a dinner party hosted by Faulkner's friend Ella Somerville. The
next day, at Faulkner's invitation, Welty and Robinson drove out to Sardis Lake and
went sailing with him on his craft, the* Ring Dove. *Neither writer made any mention
of the postcard Faulkner had sent to Welty from Hollywood six years earlier.*

*Below is a passage from a letter Welty wrote to the novelist Jean Stafford on
September 2, 1949, telling of the memorable encounter.*

JOHN ROBINSON is here in Jackson too and we had a good weekend in
Oxford, Miss., last weekend—visiting friends who fed us on pheasants—and
William Faulkner took us sailing on his sailboat on a big inland lake they've
cut out of the woods there—waves and everything, big. We were late getting
there—got lost and went to Blackjack, Miss.—and when we found the lake
there was Faulkner, cruising around, and headed right for us, through the
dead cypresses and stumps and all, pulled down his sail and took the oar, and

hollered, "You all better take your shoes off and get ready to wade," which we did, sinking—got pulled on board and then we sailed all around, all quiet and nice—what a wonderful person he is, the most profound face, something that nearly breaks your heart though, just in the clasp of his hand—a strange kind of life he leads in Oxford, two lives really. We never, either time I've been with him, talked about anything bookish of course—it's his life, not his opinions,—that seems to be with you all the time. He can do or make anything, and can sail beautifully. We got in his 20 year old Ford touring car which he hunts and fishes and goes over the farm in, with holes in the floor ("well, I know where the holes are") and when we couldn't open a back door he said, "There's a cupboard latch on it," you ought to see that car.

Faulkner in his sailboat, *Ring Dove,* on Sardis Lake

Review of Intruder in the Dust
[1949]

This review of Faulkner's Intruder in the Dust *was published as "In Yoknapataw-pha" in* Hudson Review, *1 (Winter 1949), pp. 596–98.*

WHAT GOES ON here? Grave-digging. "Digging and undigging." What's in the grave? One body or maybe another, maybe nothing at all—except human shame, something we've done to ourselves. Who digs? Who but the innocent, the young—and the old and female, their burning-up energy generating a radiance over Yoknapatawpha County and its concerns? Not forgetting the Gowrie twins—like the vaudeville team that follows behind the beautiful stars with its hilarious, mechanical parody, the Gowries from the hills dig too.

Intruder in the Dust is a story of the proving of innocence, this proof a maddening physical labor and a horrendous, well-nigh impossible undertaking, full of riddles and always starting over. The real innocents are the provers, the technical innocent is old, black Lucas Beauchamp in danger of lynching for murder of a white man—and Lucas is a lightless character, high-and-mighty and gorgeously irritating, who would be so temptingly guilty if he weren't so irrevocably innocent, just the kind of man to get in just this kind of fix, who has been building up to it all his life, and now, by hints, condescends to be saved, offering cash fees, and requiring a receipt. The provers, exhumers that they have to be, are Miss Eunice Habersham, "a practical woman" in her seventies, who "hadn't taken long . . . to decide that the way to get a dead body up out of a grave was to go out to the grave and dig it up," and the sixteen-year-olds, Charles Mallison, white, Aleck Sander, colored, who end up dog-tired and a step along in man's wisdom. Gavin Stevens, the articulate uncle who by his character partly forecasts and foretells for Charles, and the sighing mother—wonderfully done—are near at hand, summoned or pushed back, and beyond and dipping down is the menacing fringe of the Gowries from the ridges of wild Beat Four. Out of the diggings comes a solution and an indictment, defining a hope, prayer, that we should one day reach that point where it will be *Thou shalt not kill at all*, where Lucas Beauchamp's life will be secure not despite the fact that he is Lucas Beauchamp but because he is.

The action of *Intruder* is frantic—and meditative, not missing a minute. The more-than-possible failure of the task overhangs it like a big cliff. The suspense is of the chase—sometimes slow-motion, sometimes double-time; leg-work, horses, mules ("unspookable" for this business), pickup trucks, on up to a fast Sheriff's auto, bear the characters toward their grave-robbing with greater and greater urgency. The setting is the open country at night lighted by a "thin distillation of starlight," and a few dusky interiors, smelly. (How Faulkner can show us that making things out in the dark is a quality of perception as well as a quantity!) In counterpoint is the Square, back in Jefferson, with the face of its crowd, the immobile, inflexible crowd around which sentience strives and threads and skirts, until the crowd's final whizzing away like a battery of witches on brooms. Even when old Man Gowrie gets his Vinson back, brushes the quicksand off and takes him home to bury again tomorrow, is this story going to stop? "This time Hampton and his uncle could go out there tomorrow night and dig him up" is the boy's sleepy valediction that night.

Intruder is marvelously funny. Faulkner's veracity and accuracy about the world around keeps the comic thread from ever being lost or fouled, but that's a simple part of the matter. The complicated and intricate thing is that his stories aren't decked out in humor, but the humor is born in them, as much their blood and bones as the passion and poetry. Put one of his stories into a single factual statement and it's pure outrage—so would life be—too terrifying, too probable and too symbolic too, too funny to bear. There has to be the story, to bear it—wherein that statement, conjured up and implied and demonstrated, not said or the sky would fall on our heads, is yet the living source of his comedy—and a good part of that comedy's adjoining terror, of course.

It doesn't follow that *Intruder*, short, funny, of simple outline, with its detective-story casing, is one of the less difficult of Faulkner's novels. Offering side-by-side variations of numerous words, daringly long, building ever-working sentences (longer than "The Bear"'s, maybe, if anybody is counting), moods and moments arrested, pulled up to peaks, willfully crowned with beauty and terror and surprise and comedy, Faulkner has at once reexplored his world with his marvelous style that can always search in new ways, and also appeared to use from beginning to end the prerogatives of an impromptu piece of work. It could be that to seem impromptu is an illusion great art can always give as long as profundities of theme, organization and passionate content can come at a calling, but the art of what other has these cadenzas? Even the witty turns and the perfect neatness of plot look like the marks of a flash inspiration. If *Intruder* did come intruding in a literal way, shaped from the dust into life before the eyes, then we have a special wonder here; but it's none of our business, and the important thing is the wonder, special or not.

Time shifts its particles over a scene now and then, past and future like seasoning from a shaker, and Yoknapatawpha County we know now too, while the new story in its year, month, and ticking hour of day and night, emerges in that illumination and shading which Faulkner supplies to the last inch and the ultimate moment. The political views in *Intruder*, delivered outright as a speech, are made, rightly enough, another such shading to the story.

As in all Faulkner's work, the separate scenes leap up on their own, we progress as if by bonfires lighted on the way, and the essence of each scene takes form before the eyes, a shape in the fire. We see in matchless, "substituteless" (Faulkner's word for swearing) actuality and also by its contained vision: "Miss Habersham's round hat on the exact top of her head such as few people had seen in fifty years and probably no one at any time looking up out of a halfway rifled grave." Every aspect of vision is unique, springs absolute out of the material and the moment, only nominally out of "character" or "point of view," and so we see hats and happenings and every other thing, if not upward from a half-rifled grave, then down the road of the dark shuttered cabins, or up a jail stair, from the lonely ridge where Gowries come; or see in accompaniment with the smell of quicksand (a horse is there to get the smell and rear up), by the light even of impending conflagrations. Old Man Gowrie turning over a body that's the wrong body, not his son's, becomes "only an old man for whom grief was not even a component of his own but merely a temporary phenomenon of his slain son, jerking a strange corpse over onto its back not in appearance to its one mute indicting cry not for pity not for vengeance not for justice but just to be sure he had the wrong one, crying cheery abashless and loud, 'Yep it's that damned Montgomery damned if it ain't!'" The boy's feverish dream of Miss Habersham trying to drive around the mob to get back to her own house, a vision of How the Old Woman Got Home, is this writer's imagination soaring like the lark.

Of course it's a feat, this novel—a double and delightful feat, because the mystery of the detective-story plot is being raveled out while the mystery of Faulkner's prose is being spun and woven before our eyes. And with his first novel in eight years, the foremost critics are all giving cries as if (to change the image) to tree it. It's likely that Faulkner's prose can't be satisfactorily analyzed and accounted for, until it can be predicted, God save the day. Faulkner's prose, let's suspect, is intolerantly and intolerably unanalyzable and quite pure, something more than a possum in a tree—with its motes bright-pure and dark-pure falling on us, critics and non-critics alike.

Letter in Defense of Faulkner
[1949]

On October 23, 1948, the New Yorker *published Edmund Wilson's unfavorable review of Faulkner's* Intruder in the Dust. *On January 1, 1949, in a letter to the magazine's "Department of Amplification," Eudora Welty came to Faulkner's defense.*

Jackson, Mississippi
December 15, 1948
To the Editors, *The New Yorker,*
Gentlemen:

HOW WELL Illinois or South Dakota or Vermont has fared in *The New Yorker* book-review column lately, I haven't noticed, but Mississippi was pushed under three times in two weeks, and I am scared we are going to drown, if we know enough to.

It's that combination "intelligent . . . despite" that we're given as a verdict each time. The "intelligent" refers to the books or their characters and the "despite" refers to the authors' living in Mississippi. Now there's one who is not only intelligent despite, but, it appears, not quite intelligent enough because of. In fact, one of this country's most highly respected critics writes three or four pages in a recent *New Yorker* on one of the great writers and begrudges him his greatness, and I do feel like "noticing."

Edmund Wilson, reviewing *Intruder in the Dust,* by William Faulkner, reaches one of his chief points in the paragraph:

To be thus out of date, as a Southerner, in feeling and in language and in human relations, is for a novelist, a source of strength. But Faulkner's weakness has also its origin in the antiquated community he inhabits, for it consists in his not having mastered—I speak of the design of his books as wholes as well as of that of his sentences and paragraphs—the discipline of the Joyces, Prousts, and Conrads (though Proust had his solecisms and what the ancients called anacolutha). If you are going to do embroidery, you have to watch every stitch; if you are going to construct a complex machine, you have to have every part tested. The technique of the modern novel, with its ideal of technical efficiency, its specialization of means for ends, has grown up in the industrial age, and it has a good deal in common with the other manifestations of that age. In practicing it so far from such cities as produced the Flauberts, Joyces, and Jameses, Faulkner's provinciality, stubbornly cherished and turned into an asset, inevitably tempts him to be slipshod and has apparently made it impossible for him to acquire complete expertness in an art that demands of the artist the closest attention and care.

That last sentence, born in New York, has the flaw of a grammatical mistake; I don't know what being out of date in feeling means; and I didn't mind looking up "anacolutha"—but to get through to the point, *Intruder in the Dust* itself having been forgotten earlier in the piece, I shy at this idea of novel writing as a competitive, up-to-the-minute technical industry, if only for the picture it gives me of Mr. Faulkner in a striped cloth cap, with badge and lunchbox, marching in to match efficiency with the rest only to have Boss Man Wilson dock him—as an example, too—for slipshod bolt-and-nut performance caused by unsatisfactory home address. Somehow, I feel nobody could go on from there, except S. J. Perelman, and he works in another department.

It's as though we were told to modify our opinion of Cézanne's painting because Cézanne lived not in Paris but by preference in Aix and painted Aix apples—"stubbornly" (what word could ever apply less to the quality of the imagination's working?).

Such critical irrelevance, favorable or unfavorable, the South has long been used to, but now Mr. Wilson fancies it up and it will resound a little louder. Mr. Faulkner all the while continues to be capable of passion, of love, of wisdom, perhaps of prophecy, toward his material. Isn't that enough? Such qualities can identify themselves anywhere in the world and in any century without furnishing an address or references. Should this disconcert the critic who cannot or does not write without furnishing his? Well, maybe it should.

Mr. Wilson has to account for the superior work of Mr. Faulkner, of course he has to, and to show why the novelist writes his transcendent descriptions, he offers the explanation that the Southern man-made world is different looking, hence its impact is different, and those adjectives come out. (Different looking—to whom?) Could the simple, though superfluous, explanation not be that the recipient of the impact, Mr. Faulkner, is the different component here, possessing the brain as he does, and that the superiority of the work done lies in that brain?

Mr. Faulkner (if report of his custom is true) has probably not bothered to look at the reviews of his book; he certainly doesn't need a defender of any sort; but it's hard to listen to anyone being condescended to, and to a great man being condescended to pretentiously. Nearly all writers in the world live, or in their day lived, out of the U.S. North and the U.S. South alike, taking them by and large and over random centuries. (Only Mr. Wilson is counting for the city vs. the country, to my sketchy knowledge.) And it does seem that in criticizing a novel there could be more logic and purity of judgment than Mr. Wilson shows in pulling out a map. In final estimate he places

Faulkner up with the great, as well he might, but with a corrective tap asks him—maybe twice—to stand on just a little lower step for the group picture, to bring out a point in the composition. I still don't think the picture turned out too clear, somebody was bound to move.

For of course there's such a thing as a literary frame of reference that isn't industrial New York City in 1948, just as there's a literary frame through which one can look and not find "pages" of Mr. Faulkner's "The Bear" "almost opaque." "Opaque"—to whom? To Mr. Wilson I would say that I believe they are clear to me (for one example—((queer eyesight and all))), remembering too that each of us is just one looker. The important thing is that Mr. Faulkner's pages are here to look *at*.

Yours sincerely,
Eudora Welty

Faulkner's "The Bear"
[1949]

The following discussion of Faulkner's "The Bear" began as part of a lecture given at the University of Washington and was first published, heavily revised, in the Atlantic *(1949) as "The Reading and Writing of Short Stories." Welty examines the plots in stories by Stephen Crane, Katherine Mansfield, Ernest Hemingway, Anton Chekhov, D. H. Lawrence, and William Faulkner and shows how each writer creates a fictional world that is individual, distinct, and unique. In a long discussion of Lawrence's "The Fox," she reveals how Lawrence's world is built on sensation. She exemplifies the world of Faulkner, a "divining" writer, with "The Bear."*

This excerpt is taken from a final revised version, "Looking at Short Stories," collected in Welty's The Eye of the Story: Selected Essays & Reviews, *New York: Random House, 1978, pp. 61–81.*

"THE BEAR" begins:

> There was a man and a dog too this time. Two beasts, counting Old Ben the bear, and two men, counting Boon Hogganbeck, in whom some of the same blood ran which ran in Sam Fathers, even though Boon's was a plebeian strain of it and in only Sam and Old Ben and the mongrel Lion was taintless and incorruptible.

And we're in a different world. There is a world outside, which we're expected to be acquainted with in its several stratifications, to which our inner world communicates and to which it answers. The blood in this story may not be conscious or unconscious, but it can be *tainted*—that is, it can be considered in its relation to action, to opinion, to life going on outside. Blood can be plebeian, mongrel, taintless, incorruptible in one sentence of William Faulkner's, whereas in all of Lawrence it is one thing, the abode of the unconscious.

You will remember that this is a hunting story. A boy has known always of a great bear in the hunting country he was born into; encounters the bear after his initiation into the wilderness, and does not kill him; but at last, years later, with a beast that is trained to be his match (the mongrel, Lion), the fatal encounter takes place, and bear, dog and old pure-blooded Indian all die of it.

We see at once as we read that this narrative has the quality of happening, and the blood of inheriting; the story indeed has signs of having so much to do with the outer world that it can happen, and has happened, more than once. In one respect, this story is a sample of that happening which is continuous, indigenous to the time and the place and the human element in and through which it happens.

Ike McCaslin, in whose experience at various stages we are told the story,

realized later that it had begun long before that. It had already begun on that day when he first wrote his age in two ciphers and his cousin McCaslin brought him for the first time to the camp, the big woods, to earn for himself from the wilderness the name and state of hunter provided he in his turn were humble and enduring enough.

Humble and enduring—qualities that apply to our relationship with the world.

He had already inherited then, without ever having seen it, the big old bear with
one trap-ruined foot that in an area of almost a hundred square miles had earned
for himself a name, a definite designation like a living man—the long legend of
corncribs broken down and rifled, of shoats and grown pigs and even calves carried bodily into the woods and devoured, and traps and deadfalls overthrown and
dogs mangled and slain, and shotgun and even rifle shots delivered at pointblank
range yet with no more effect than so many peas blown through a tube by a child—
a corridor of wreckage and destruction beginning back before the boy was born,
through which sped, not fast but rather with the ruthless and irresistible delibera-
tion of a locomotive, the shaggy tremendous shape. It ran in his knowledge before
he ever saw it. It loomed and towered in his dreams before he ever saw the unaxed
woods where it left its crooked print, shaggy, tremendous, red-eyed, not malevo-
lent but just big, too big for the dogs which tried to bay it, for the horses which
tried to ride it, for the men and the bullets they fired into it; too big for the very
country which was its constricting scope.

See the outer edges of this bear becoming abstract—but this bear is not
the fox. "It was as if the boy had already divined what his senses and intellect
had not encompassed yet. . . ."

For this bear belongs to the world, the world of experience:

that doomed wilderness whose edges were being constantly and punily gnawed at
by men with plows and axes who feared it because it was wilderness, men myriad
and nameless even to one another in the land where the old bear earned a name,
and through which ran not even a mortal beast but an anachronism indomitable
and invincible out of an old, dead time, a phantom, epitome and apotheosis of the
old, wild life which the little puny humans swarmed and hacked at in a fury of
abhorrence and fear, like pygmies about the ankles of a drowsing elephant;—the

old bear, solitary, indomitable, and alone; widowered, childless, and absolved of mortality—old Priam, reft of his old wife, and outliving all his sons.

Experience in the world is the very thread this story is put together with. Here is the footprint:

> Then, standing beside Sam in the thick great gloom of ancient wood and the winter's dying afternoon, he looked quietly down at the rotted log scored and gutted with claw marks and, in the wet earth beside it, the print of the enormous warped two-toed foot. . . . For the first time he realized that the bear which had run in his listening and loomed in his dreams since before he could remember, and which therefore must have existed in the listening and the dreams of his cousin and Major de Spain and even old General Compson before they began to remember in their turn, was a mortal animal and that they had departed for the camp each November with no actual intention of slaying it, not because it could not be slain but because so far they had no actual hope of being able to.

Faulkner achieves the startling reality and nearness of the outside world by alternately dilating reality to the reach of abstraction and bringing it home with a footprint. It is reality that not only *is*, but *looms*—and this not just one time to one character, but over and over, with an insistent quality.

There are several encounters between Ike McCaslin and the bear. The final one is a death struggle when the bear is

> on its hind feet, its back against a tree while the bellowing hounds swirled around it and once more Lion [the mongrel dog that is his match] drove in, leaping clear of the ground. This time the bear didn't strike him down. It caught the dog in both arms, almost loverlike, and they both went down.

There is a terrible fight, Lion clings to the bear's throat and the bear tears at Lion's body and wounds him mortally, but Lion will not let go. Boon, Lion's trainer who loves him, when Lion is clawed, runs toward them, a knife in his hand. He flings himself astride the bear and the knife falls.

> It fell just once. . . . The bear then surged erect, raising with it the man and the dog too, and turned and still carrying the man and the dog it took two or three steps towards the woods on its hind feet as a man would have walked and crashed down. It didn't collapse, crumple. It fell all of a piece, as a tree falls, so that all three of them, man, dog and bear, seemed to bounce once.

The bear and the dog die of this, and so does Sam Fathers, the Indian, who is found lying motionless face down in the trampled mud when it's all over: not a mark on him, "he just quit." The bodies of the bear and Sam, open-eyed, teeth bared, brown—childless, kinless, peopleless—are stretched out alike.

"The Bear" ends with the death of three and a falling tree, as, you remember, "The Fox" ended—if you count the life-in-death of March and Henry as one death shared. The tree in Faulkner's story, along with the dying bear and his burden of victim and killer, is a wilderness falling. The fox is a denizen of the inner world, purely. The bear is, equally purely, of the outer world—not simply the material, three-dimensional outer world, which is good enough, but the measureless outer world of experience, the knowing and sentient past, the wisdom of Time and Place. Both bear and fox are vanquished by acts of the destructive will of man's aggression. But Faulkner's battles, taking place in an ever-present physical territory which now and again is also some projected country of the spirit, are conscious battles. Faulkner deals with such aspects of the human being as dignity and glory and corruptibility and incorruptibility and ridicule and defeat and pride and endurance—especially endurance, a word that might as well be in Cherokee to Lawrence. Lawrence's battles are won and lost in the "blood conscious- ness." It's as if the two worlds of Faulkner and Lawrence were, here, the inside-out of each other.

Faulkner seems to me, rather than an intuitive writer, a divining one. And his stories seem to race with time, race with the world, in an indirect ratio, perhaps, to the length of his sentences. The sixteen-thousand-word sentence in "The Bear" races like a dinosaur across the early fields of time. It runs along with a strange quality of seeming all to happen at once. It makes us realize once again that prose is a structure in its every part, that the imagi- nation is engineered when we write. A sentence may be in as perfect control as a church or a bridge.

"The Bear" is an apocalyptic story of the end of the wilderness. It ends with the senseless clang on clang of a man idiotically pounding pieces of his bro- ken gun together while in the isolated gum tree over his head forty or fifty squirrels are running frantically round and round. It signifies, for one thing, the arrival of the machine age and the squealing treadmill. This story encom- passes past and future, all the past of the land from Indian times on to now. It has towering heroic figures, wilderness figures, symbolic figures; and through the hunter—whom we see in the present, in boyhood, the past, the future, in ancestry (in the ledgers and memories and paraphernalia of the place)—we are aware in every happening of its power to happen again, over and over; we are aware of the whole world of the wilderness, the whole his- tory of Mississippi.

For in "The Bear," the structure of time is constantly in danger of being ripped away, torn down by the author; the *whole* time bulges, tries to get into the present-time of the story. This dilation in time sense and intractability in space sense, the whole surface of the story, has of itself a kind of looming quality, a portentousness. Like the skin of a balloon, time and space are stretched to hold more and more, while the story still holds it as long as it can, and in both form and function it dangerously increases.

And in Part Four of this long story the flimsy partition that keeps the story-time apart from whole time is allowed to fly away entirely. So the entire history of the land and a people crowds into a chapter whose expansion, in sentence and paragraph, is almost outrageous to the eye alone. Time and space have been too well invoked, and they tear through the story running backward and forward, up and down and around, like a pack of beasts themselves out of the world's wilderness. And this is the beauty of the story. Its self-destruction, self-immolation, is the way the story transcends all it might have been had it stayed intact and properly nailed together. There is the wonder.

Of course, such transcending might belong to some subjects and to other subjects it would bring foolishness. It the case of "The Bear" we can assume that to Faulkner the escapement of wild time and place seemed one attribute of the thing he was writing about—the lost attribute, implicit in it, and supplied now, in his story. In letting time and place out of the box he was not, by any standards but our ordinary ones, being reckless. By his own, he was being true, faithful to his composition of the story at hand. There is no other integrity.

Presentation Speech:
The Gold Medal for Fiction
[1962]

At the annual meeting of the National Institute of Arts and Letters, Eudora Welty, a member of the Institute and Faulkner's fellow Mississippian, presented the gold medal to him for his lifetime achievement. Her remarks and Faulkner's words of acceptance, printed following hers, are from the Proceedings of the American Academy of Arts and Letters and the National Institute of Arts and Letters, *Second Series, Number Thirteen, New York 1963.*

MR. FAULKNER, your work and our love for it have both been alive for a long time now, as your work will be after we are not. A medal may not last nearly so long, yet its worth is that it too is a word, greatness said out loud. A medal is a word that can be held in the hand, taken by some appointed hand and put into the hand it belongs to.

Saying greatness, and when we know there is no mistake, we praise ourselves too, can't help it or wish to help it. Now it is so clear as to be demonstrated that we believe ourselves able to accommodate yours, to declare it out of our own hearts. The world is never asked to give art a medal, and never will be asked. For, as we here know, art has so little to do, in its processes as in its very start, with claims on anything; has only to do each time with one man's unaided seeing of the world, shaping his work to what he by himself

William Faulkner and Eudora Welty with the Gold Medal for Fiction. In deference to the recipient, Welty gave it to him privately before going to the stage and presented only the empty case in the public ceremony, 1962.

sees and sees into. We have not, as your readers, been asked for anything, but we have been—and this truly is staggering—communicated with, and the subject is, always has been and will be, life. A big demand *has* been made, the biggest of all. Your work by simply existing is a claim without a stop, made on our understanding.

The most evident thing in all our minds at this moment must be that your fictional world, with its tragedy, its beauty, its hilarity, its long passion, its generations of feeling and knowing, the whole of your extraordinary world, is alive and in the room here and with us now. We inhabit it; and so will they, each one for himself, the readers in days to come. We all inhabit it all, and this is because your work, a triumphant vision, inhabits us, includes us. In its long persisting, it increases us. And so literally our hearts may accommodate, now, something they could not have done before you wrote your books. That your fiction can and does go on and on revealing human life is a fact itself revealed through us each time we read, as we find again your vision enveloping us like new, to bring us again inside experience we had already known was indelible.

Mr. Faulkner, I think this medal, being pure of its kind, the real gold, would go to you of its own accord, and know its owner regardless of whether we were all here to see or not. Safe as a puppy it would climb into your pocket. But the ceremony is our part of the medal, and to my own everlasting pride and pleasure the Institute has given me the honor of presenting it: to Mr. William Faulkner, from the National Institute of Arts and Letters, The Gold Medal for Fiction.

ACCEPTANCE BY MR. FAULKNER

Miss Welty, Mr. President, Members of the Academy, Ladies and Gentlemen: This award has, to me, a double value. It is not only a comforting recognition of some considerable years of reasonably hard and arduous, anyway consistently dedicated, work. It also recognizes and affirms, and so preserves, a quantity in our American legend and dream well worth preserving.

I mean a quantity in our past: that past which was a happier time in the sense that we were innocent of many of the strains and anguishes and fears which these atomic days have compelled on us. This award evokes the faded airs and dimming rotogravures which record that vanished splendor still inherent in the names of Saint Louis and Leipzig, the quantity which they celebrated and signified recorded still today in the labels of wine bottles and ointment jars.

I think that those gold medals, royal and unique above the myriad spawn of their progeny which were the shining ribbons fluttering and flashing among the booths and stalls of forgotten county fairs in recognition and accolade of a piece of tatting or an apple pie, did much more than record a victory. They affirmed the premise that there are no degrees of best; that one man's best is the equal of any other best, no matter how asunder in time or space or comparison, and should be honored as such.

We should keep that quantity, more than ever now, when roads get shorter and easier between aim and gain and goals become less demanding and more easily attained, and there is less and less space between elbows and more and more pressure on the individual to relinquish into one faceless serration like a mouthful of teeth, simply in order to find room to breathe. We should remember those times when the idea of an individuality of excellence compounded of resourcefulness and independence and uniqueness not only deserved a blue ribbon but got one. Let the past abolish the past when—and if—it can substitute something better; not us to abolish the past simply because it was.

Memorial Tribute: Author Gave Life to Fictional County [1962]

William Faulkner died on July 6, 1962. Eudora Welty wrote this valediction at the request of the Associated Press news service. It was printed in, among other newspapers, the Washington Post/Times Herald, *July 7, 1962, p. 2C.*

WILLIAM FAULKNER saw all the world in his fictional county where we can see it now—where he made it live. His work is a triumphant vision. This vision, like life itself, has its light and dark, its time and place, and love and battle, its generations of feeling, and its long reaches of what happens to people out there and inside, in heart and mind, which is so much.

Of course he wrote what was more, and will remain more, than others knew before him; he has instructed as well as moved and amazed us, a great artist.

So unmistakenly born out of knowledge of his own, out of sense and feeling (love, apprehension, outrage, compassion, pride, grief) for his own, his novels and stories were built at every step and stage out of his long passion of seeing the life he knew by seeing as well as he could into it and around it.

All this required, and took, an imagination that has shone incomparably the brightest in our firmament.

What is great and puny, what is tragic and uproarious about us all in our own dogged lives everywhere, is a living life itself on any page of his. And in literature it is this that matters and always will matter.

Humanity was his subject, but he was a poet when he was born to see what he saw. Laid, nearly all of it at home in Mississippi, his work has a poet's authority by which it travels the world and puts the world to measure. Indeed, these days, it seems itself when the world does not.

We have learned lately that it sank into the bones of the Japanese as readily as into ours here. Though once you could buy his books in France, I believe, and not in New York, except with luck at second-hand, and not anywhere in Jackson, Miss.

Surely he never wrote a line except what his own eyes, ears, memory and his poet's imagination told him what was not "true" but truth.

He went out on every limb, I believe, that he knew was there.

Keynote Speech: Southern Literary Festival [1965]

This address, never before published, was presented by Welty as the keynote speech at the Southern Literary Festival held at the University of Mississippi in April 1965. It is transcribed from her original manuscript in the Eudora Welty Collection of the Mississippi Department of Archives and History. The festival was convened in Faulkner's hometown and in his honor. He had died three years earlier. Besides Welty's, there were presentations by the writers Malcolm Cowley and Robert Penn Warren and by the actress Ruth Ford. Welty was present for the unveiling of Leon Koury's bronze sculpture of Faulkner, and for the first time she was able to visit Rowan Oak, Faulkner's home, opened briefly to the public during the conference.

WE ARE GATHERED here today for the opening of the Southern Literary Festival in the town of our greatest writer where he from the age of five made his home, which he loved throughout his life, and where he died. A program of lectures by three distinguished visitors who knew him and his work intimately—two who have written about it to our great reward, one who has performed it on the stage—is to begin a short while from now. We are first to hear Mr. Cowley tell us about the putting together and the editing of *The Portable Faulkner*. This evening we shall hear one of the first and another one of the best critics of William Faulkner when Mr. Warren speaks. Tomorrow

45

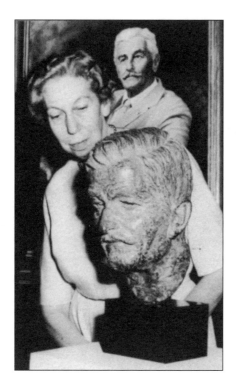

we are to hear Miss Ruth Ford tell about her experience in adapting and playing the leading role in the Broadway production of *Requiem for a Nun*. Besides, during the day, in the finely stocked and finely kept Mississippi Room in the University Library Miss Oldham will show us the shelves of Mr. Faulkner's books, in their first editions and in many translations, and perhaps let us see a page or two of manuscript. At the Mary Buie Museum we can see on view the Nobel Prize, the Legion of Honor, and other prizes. An exhibition of photographs of Faulkner Country is hanging; there will be shown a documentary film written by our Festival president of this year, Mr. Harrington.

The home of William Faulkner is to be open today and tomorrow to the members of the Festival. We may go inside, visit the study where he worked; stroll under the trees, hear the birds, go around to the backyard where he liked to go and sit; the rosebushes that he planted and worked and saw bloom ought now to be just about coming into leaf—maybe, too, the big pear tree that fell in a storm, which I was told he gently propped up and made survive.

Thus we shall be everywhere in the presence of our great writer. We already are. It is a presence that is already here, that presides here, and so there was never a need for us to begin by invoking it. Without the slightest effort on our part William Faulkner is present today.

Present in his life's work.

Do we not feel the physical nearness of it all? From where we are it seems that we could walk to the golf course that used to be the Compson's pasture, where *The Sound and the Fury* opens; and we must have already been, by now, around the Courthouse Square where it ends.

We are surrounded by other places we know as well as Jefferson, some set back a little way and some very far indeed in distance or in time. It was southeast of us, I believe, before they cut it down—the vast uncharted tract of wilderness where Old Ben ran in the days of Sam Fathers. Closer by, in the hill country, stands Will Varner's store, the "knife-gnawed wooden bench" on the gallery, the "heel-gnawed steps," the teams and saddled horses and mules hitched to the posts, and probably V. K. Ratliff's buckboard with them and his "sturdy, mismatched team." (There's as much mismatching going on in Faulkner as there is twinning.) We can see the whittlers on the gallery. And up at Varner's house we can see Eula looking out of the window. Mrs. Littlejohn comes out of her kitchen and stands at her washline to look at *us*. We have, indelibly, been to Frenchman's Bend. We have seen the entrance and the exit of the Spotted Horses.

Comedy has raced how often through this countryside, and around this Square too. And tragedy's inside the houses. There is the Compson interior. It is a grey night of moonlight, the one when the honeysuckle drizzled, and Quentin is lying on his bed wanting it to stop. Behind the house and across the ditch, in another interior, is Nancy, some years earlier, sitting in the open and unprotected, lit-up doorway, waiting for her husband to come and kill her. Inside the Reverend Hightower's kitchen, Joe Christmas is crouched behind the table, waiting with his hands in chains, "bright and glittering," "resting upon the upper edge," as Percy Grim arrives with his automatic.

I believe it takes an enormous respect for the outside world to understand, and then to show, what lies behind it and what has made it that way. Mr. Faulkner seemed to me to look at the world with the eyes of a man who likes making things. We remember how, if he ever was brought to speak of himself as a writer at work, it was as a good carpenter selecting the best materials to hand and turning them with the right tools. We can accept this straight, it seems to me. Cash Bundren, the carpenter son in *As I Lay Dying*, says it's "better to build a tight chicken coop than a shoddy courthouse," and when he falls off the church roof he is perfectly well able to estimate the distance as "twenty-eight foot, four and a half inches, about."

Faulkner had exactness. He couldn't have shot the moon without it. You can only swing the extravagant and wonderful arc when you hold in your hand the sharp, plain fact. One of the earliest things we know about Flem Snopes, of measureless meanness, is the measurement of that snap-on bow-tie he wore—it was two inches across, and it cost ten cents.

In the way he showed us the physical world, Mr. Faulkner was making us aware, all the time, of what made it go. Around the Square he led his procession, performing its antics, driven by its suffering; through his marvelous ear he could hear and could tell us what all of them said. And out of *his* heart he knew what they were saying in their hearts as well.

Here in Oxford this morning we shall feel ourselves deeply susceptible, I think, to more than place. We shall feel susceptible to time too. William Faulkner's work, as we know, was saturated with both.

The thing we know most immediately after *where* we are is *when*—the hour and the day and the season. Whatever season it is in a story by William Faulkner, I believe that's the only time in the world there is. He loved the Mississippi spring:

"In the woods the tree frogs were going, smelling rain in the air; they sounded like toy music boxes that were hard to turn."

In the "dreaming lambence of the moonlight beyond the veranda, the pear tree across the road opposite was now in full bloom," its twigs and branches "standing motionless and perpendicular above the horizontal boughs like the separate and upstreaming hair of a drowned woman sleeping upon the uttermost floor of the windless and tideless sea." (That's in Frenchman's Bend.)

William Faulkner has worked and reworked the stuff of time in its happening. Here in this historic town, it doesn't seem strange, if it ever did, that this fiction in rising as if spontaneously out of place, got itself finally organized around time. It seems entirely appropriate to the place and the stories that they proceeded and increased by moving and turning around one fixed point in the local history, then another.

Yoknapatawpha is mappable—and we are to hear about the map that was made for *The Portable Faulkner*, I hope, when Mr. Cowley speaks on that volume later in the day. In general I would say that the geography of novels is mappable after the fact. Yoknapatawpha, more so than the scene of any fiction that readily comes to mind, has place, and the place in turn has past, present and future; it is subject to time, to change, and carries its own memory along with it. One glory of Faulkner's world is its quality of happening, the reach and sweep and scope and drive of human experience taking place in it. This intensity of life is the stuff of which fiction's map is made, for human passion is the real territory. Jefferson, Frenchman's Bend, Sutpen's Hundred—every place name that studs and stars it—are evidence of this passion, its cause and result.

Walking through these lovely and history-laden streets, we feel ourselves deeply susceptible also to the *intimate* aspects of time—to the common memory. Remembering is so basic and vital a part of existence in the Faulkner stories that it takes on the strength of instinct and acquires the power of hallucination. Remembering is done through the blood, is a physical absorption through the body; it can be inherited, he makes us believe. Again, it's a spiritual heritage—blessing or curse. All the way through his work, memory asserts its role vocally and inwardly—and has, perhaps, the final answer. The great role memory plays in his work never seemed strange in the reading. Here in Oxford we recognize it as if in person; remembering is taken for granted, is a way of living utterly familiar.

In *Light in August* Mr. Faulkner says: "Memory believes before knowing remembers." I believe it's safe to say that *time*, to this writer, was in the long run *human* time.

When a student at the University of Virginia asked Mr. Faulkner why his sentences were so long, he got this reply:

"To me, no man is himself, he is the sum of his past. There is no such thing really as *was*, because the past *is*. It is a part of every man, every woman, every moment. All of his and her ancestry, background, is all a part of himself and herself at any moment. And so a man, a character in a story at any moment of action, is not just himself as he is then, he is all that made him; and the long sentence is an attempt to get his past and possibly his future into the instant in which he does something . . ."

And so we have Compsons, McCaslins, Sartorises, Sutpens, Snopeses—and the others. I can't estimate the count, but I would use a Faulkner word and call them myriad: farmers, Indians, Sunday School teachers, doctors, blacksmiths, merchants, mule traders, carnival pitchmen, jurists, band leaders, sawmill planers, livery hands, hunters, ministers, dipsomaniacs, schoolteachers, sheriffs, yarn-spinners, carpenters, convicts, officers, and soldiers of the Confederacy and every other war, imbeciles, boardinghouse-keepers, wanderers, cooks, users of divining rods, horse-thieves and barn burners and Phi Beta Kappas. They are white, Negro, Indian, Chinese, Huguenot, Scotch, English, Spanish, French, or any combination of these, and known always or at any point of their time on earth from birth till death and in between.

It is another population of this town and county—its co-existent inhabitants, whose history has been their history. It is a population that has *reality* as distinguished from *actuality*: they are our hearts made visible and audible and above all dramatic; they are ourselves translated, and, at times, transmogrified. Noble and base, they speak to us; we recognize them.

Lena Grove, Miss Habersham, Jason Compson, Byron Bunch, V. K. Ratliff, Dilsey, Dewey Dell Bundren, Uncle Buck and Uncle Buddy McCaslin, Miss Emily Grierson, Henry Armstid, Miss Everbe Corinthia Hogganbeck, Major De Spain—any name, any one living character, calls up in the mind a story, a novel, a cluster and congregation of both, the sum of everybody.

We know the animals too—Old Ben and Lion, Miss Reba Rivers' two dogs "Mr. Binford" and "Miss Reba"; all the dogs, all the horses. And these—"calico-coated, small-bodied, with delicate legs and pink faces in which their mismatched eyes rolled wild and subdued, . . . gaudy, motionless and alert, wild as deer, deadly as rattlesnakes, quiet as doves." ("'Them's good, gentle ponies,' the stranger said.")

Having brought ourselves to Mr. Faukner's world, we should find it an effort *not* to people it with his characters. They seem part of one identity. A more extraordinary fact is that this is the world where he thought them up, where he wrote them down. Somewhere in this vicinity, a picture, an image once came into William Faulkner's head of—I quote—"the muddy seat of a little girl's drawers when she went climbing the pear tree to look in the parlor window, to see what in the world the grown people were doing that the children couldn't see": which he has said was the beginning of Caddy—"my heart's darling"—and Caddy meant the beginning of *The Sound and the Fury*.

To be told this much about a novel's origin is quite enough—to press to know more would be to pry; and if there were any more that could be told, it is doubtful that it would explain it any better. Origins are mysterious, whatever handle you try to pick them up by. *The Sound and the Fury* gave its author the most trouble, so he said, of all his novels—he let one character try telling the story, then let another try, then another, "and then I let Faulkner try it," and the story tantalized him to the end. Naturally, it was the one of his books that remained the closest to his heart.

Here, *The Sound and the Fury* happened. That doesn't help us, but what matters in art doesn't have to help us. It is just a fact of this Festival. It is a fact that piety gets nowhere near. We should note it.

Not too many yards away from where we now sit is still a room about which the author has remarked:

"I got a job in the power plant, on the night shift, from 6 P.M. to 6 A.M., as a coal passer. I shoveled coal from the bunker into a wheelbarrow and wheeled it in and dumped it where the fireman could put it into the boiler. About 11 o'clock the people would be going to bed, and so it did not take so much steam. Then we could rest, the fireman and I. He would sit in a chair and doze. I had invented a table out of a wheelbarrow in the coal bunker, just beyond a wall from where a dynamo ran. It made a deep, constant humming noise. There was no more work to do until about 4 A.M., when we would have to clean the fires and get up steam again. On these nights, between 12 and 4, I wrote *As I Lay Dying* in six weeks, without changing a word. I sent it to Smith and wrote him that by it I would stand or fall."

Here, then, while we attend our Literary Festival and celebrate the name of William Faulkner, we have a specific opportunity—rare, and maybe unique in our country—to see spread out in one exhibition a great storyteller's material and the art he has made of it—both of them radiant and alive.

Under the spell of it all, we are free to do even such a literal thing as going around the Courthouse Square in the track course of Benjy in the final paragraph of *The Sound and the Fury*. Why not? Thereby we may prove to ourselves how much of the novel is the Courthouse Square and how much is Faulkner. Benjy lives; he lives for us not in *our* going around the Courthouse Square, but in *his*: "as cornice and facade flowed smoothly once more, from left to right: post and tree, window and doorway, and signboard, each in its ordered place." Benjy lives not in Oxford at all but in *The Sound and the Fury*. Jefferson's other name is not Oxford but the imagination of William Faulkner. It is in that original imagination and now in ours that all these unforgettable people have their true life, real meaning.

Let us not delude ourselves—because of our understandable happiness in being here—that by walking around we may run up on any reasonable or reliable explanation for William Faulkner's work. We shall only find on the home premises the greatest mystery. Here indeed is this actual world, which you and I are so hospitably invited to walk about in for a day or two while the

Festival is in progress. In the Library, tied up in a cardboard box, are some pages written in the small, neat strokes, like something made with an infinite number of little sticks all the same size, that came from his hand. And in between this town and that box stretches a distance not one of us in this room could ever cross if we tried it from now on. I don't know of anybody else alive who could do it, either.

The Oxford streets and the written page are two worlds. Standing between them, and aware that he did, lived William Faulkner. By all the effort of his life he learned and knew both worlds and he crossed that space and made the connection between them. Time and again he did it. We take it for granted because he did it, but with those tiny little strokes of the pen he was performing a feat of Hercules.

It is the feat that Mr. Faulkner described for himself when he answered a student's question at the University of Virginia about what qualities he thought imbeciles and half-wits possessed that made him use such characters in a story. "I wouldn't say that he has those qualities," said Mr. Faulkner. "That is the perogative of the writer—to use his imagination to that extent, if it makes something that seems moving and true. Maybe the imbecile *should* have that quality. That's what I mean by truth. He probably hasn't, which is the fact, but maybe he should, which is the truth."

What we see is that the actual world that gave rise to the novels is part vanished, part overlaid, part still here, part never. What we know is that, made and remade in his imagination, his created world is a real world itself, here to stay.

Everywhere around us is the original and concrete thing; but the irrefutable fact is, to begin with, he saw better than we can. And the way to see the reality is to look for it where we saw it before, in the novels and stories. Faulkner sees with the eyes of the artist and can make us see what is here

54

and at the same time see through it to the truth about it, the human truth. We see his world as it is today, April 23, 1965; William Faulkner saw it for good and all. Where it lives for us deepest is where it lived for him, in the struggle of the imagination to grasp and understand the passion of the human heart.

When the National Institute of Arts and Letters voted to award its member William Faulkner the Gold Medal for Fiction in its Ceremonial on May 24, 1962, of course another member had to present it to him. I, a fellow Mississippian, was asked to do it. As I'm sure Mr. Cowley, the Institute's president, and Mr. Warren, too, know, I was well aware, as I am now, of the honor it was to me. But there was something about being called upon the stage to give William Faulkner a medal for writing that made me afraid I might drop it. Just before we all marched in, I asked him would he mind if I kept the box but passed him the medal right now. With kindness and courtesy he replied, "If you prefer," and dropped it into his pocket.

I hope no one here will mind if I read in part now what I said then to William Faulkner's face:

"Mr. Faulkner, your work and our love for it have both been alive for a long time now, as your work will be after we are not. A medal may not last nearly so long, yet its worth is that it too is a word: *greatness* said out loud.

"*Saying* greatness, saying it when we know there is no mistake, we praise ourselves too, can't help it or wish to help it. Now it is so clear as to be demonstrated that we believe ourselves able to accommodate yours, to declare it out of our own hearts.

"The world is never asked to give art a medal, and never will be asked. For, as we here know, art has so little to do, in its processes as in its very start, with claims on anything; has only to do, each time, with one man's unaided seeing of the world, shaping his work by what he himself sees and sees into. We have not, as your readers, been asked for anything. But we have been communicated with; and the subject is, always has been and will be, life. A big demand has been made, the biggest of all. Your work, by simply existing, is a claim without a stop, made on our understanding.

"The most evident thing in all our minds at this moment must be that your fictional world, with its tragedy, its beauty, its hilarity, its long passion, its generations of feeling and knowing, the whole of your extraordinary world, is alive and in the room here and with us now. We inhabit it; and so will they, each one for himself, the readers in days to come. We all inhabit it all, and this is because your work, a triumphant vision, inhabits us, includes us. In its long persisting, it increases us.

"And so literally our hearts may accommodate, now, something they could not have done before you wrote your books. That your fiction can and does go on and on revealing human life is a fact itself revealed through us each time we read, as we find again your vision enveloping us like new, to bring us again inside experience we had already known was indelible. . . ."

Then, since he already had his medal, I gave him the box.

On Faulknerian Time
[1965]

In 1965 Eudora Welty was writer-in-residence at Millsaps College in Jackson, Mississippi. The origin of her discussion of Faulknerian time was a paper on The Sound and the Fury *that she presented in a series of seminars whose theme, the nature and meaning of time, was explored by ten speakers in the humanities and the sciences. Welty's talk focused on time in the novel, citing Faulkner's as exemplary. Her full essay, from which this excerpt is taken, was titled "Some Notes on Time in Fiction." It was first published in* Mississippi Quarterly, *26 (Fall 1973), 483–92, and thereafter in* The Eye of the Story: Selected Essays and Reviews.

WHEN PASSION comes into the telling, with a quickening of human meaning, changes take place in fictional time. Some of them are formidable.

I was recently lent a book by a student which had set itself to clear up *The Sound and the Fury* by means of a timetable; the characters' arrivals and departures, including births and deaths, were listed in schedule, with connections to and from the main points of action in the novel. What has defeated the compiler is that *The Sound and the Fury* remains, after his work as before it, approachable only as a novel. He was right, of course, in seeing time to be at the bottom of it. Time, though—not chronology.

Think of the timepieces alone. Think of only one timepiece: Dilsey has to use the Compson clock; it has only one hand. "The clock tick-tocked, solemn and profound. It might have been the dry pulse of the decaying house itself;

after a while it whirred and cleared its throat and struck." It strikes five times. "Eight o'clock," says Dilsey. Even while the clock is striking, chronology is in the act of yielding to another sort of time.

Through the telling of the story three times in succession by three different Compsons in the first-person and then once again in the third-person, we are exposed to three different worlds of memory, each moving in its own orbit. "He thirty-three," Luster says of Benjy, "thirty-three this morning," and the reply comes, "You mean he been three years old thirty years." Benjy's memory is involuntary and not conscious of sequence or connections: a stick run along the palings of a fence. But time of whatever nature leaves a residue in passing, and out of Benjy comes a wail "hopeless and prolonged. It was nothing. Just sound. It might have been all time and injustice and sorrow become vocal for an instant by a conjunction of planets."

Time to Quentin is visible—his shadow; is audible—his grandfather's watch; and it is the heavy load that has to be carried inside him—his memory. Excruciatingly conscious, possessing him in torture, that memory works in spite of him and of all he can do, anywhere he can go, this last day of his life. The particular moment in time that links him forever to the past—his world—conditions *all* time. The future may be an extension of the past where possible; the future can include memory if bearable. But time will repeatedly assault what has been intact; which may be as frail as the virginity of Caddy. If experience is now, at every stage, a tragedy of association in the memory, how is the rememberer to survive? Quentin spends his last day, as he's spent his life, answering that he is already dead. He has willed the past some quality, some power, by which it can arrest the present, try to stop it from happening; can stop it.

Who, in the swirling time of this novel, knows the actual time, and can tell the story by it? Jason, of course. He keeps track of time to the second as he keeps track of money to the penny. Time is money, says Jason. And he cheats on both and is in turn cheated by both; we see him at the end a man "sitting quietly behind the wheel of a small car, with his invisible life ravelled out about him like a worn-out sock."

By all the interior evidence, we will come nearest to an understanding of this novel through the ways it speaks to us out of its total saturation with time. We read not in spite of the eccentric handling of time, but as well as we can by the aid of it. If a point is reached in fiction where chronology has to be torn down, it must be in order to admit and make room for what matters overwhelmingly more to the human beings who are its characters.

Faulkner has crowded chronology out of the way many times to make way for memory and the life of the past, as we know, and we know for what reason. "Memory believes before knowing remembers," he says (in *Light in August*). Remembering is so basic and vital a part of staying alive that it takes on the strength of an instinct of survival, and acquires the power of art. Remembering is so basic and vital a part of staying alive that it takes on the strength of an instinct of survival, and acquires the power of an art. Remembering is done through the blood, it is a bequeathment, it takes account of what happens before a man is born as if he were there taking part. It is a physical absorption through the living body, it is a spiritual heritage. It is also a life's work.

"There is no such thing as was," Faulkner remarked in answer to a student's question as to why he wrote long sentences. "To me, no man is himself, he is the sum of his past. There is no such thing really as was, because the past is. It is a part of every man, every woman, and every moment. All of his and her ancestry, background, is all a part of himself and herself at any moment. And so a man, a character in a story at any moment in action, is not just himself as he is then, he is all that made him; and the long sentence," he adds, "is an attempt to get his past and possibly his future into the instant in which he does something . . ."

Distortion of time is a deeply conscious part of any novel's conception, is an organic part of its dramatic procedure, and throughout the novel's course it matters continuously and increasingly, and exactly as the author gives it to us. The dilations, the freezing of moments, the persistent recurrences and proliferations, all the extraordinary tamperings with time in *The Sound and the Fury*, are answers to the meaning's questions, evolving on demand. For all Faulkner does to chronological time here—he explodes it—he does nothing that does not increase the dramatic power of his story. The distortions to time give the novel its deepest seriousness of meaning, and charge it with an intense emotional power that could come from nowhere else. Time, in the result, is the living essence of *The Sound and the Fury*. It appears to stand so extremely close to the plot that, in a most extraordinary way, it almost becomes the plot itself. It *is* the portentous part; it is the plot's long reverberation. Time has taken us through every degree of the long down-spiral to the novel's meaning—into the meaning; it has penetrated its way. It has searched out every convolution of a human predicament and brought us to the findings of tragedy.

Faulkner's work is, we know, magnetized to a core of time, to his conception of it as the continuing and continuousness of man. Faulknerian time is in the most profound and irrefutable sense *human* time. (*Corruption* is that which time brings to the Compsons' lives. *Progress* is the notion of those who are going to make something out of it: "What's in it for me?" ask the Snopeses.) His deepest felt and most often repeated convictions—"They endured." "Man will prevail"—are the long-reached and never-to-be-relinquished resolutions of his passionate idea of human time. And they contain, burned into them, all the plots of Faulkner's novels and stories.

Time, in a novel, may become the subject itself. Mann, attacking the subjectivity of man's knowledge of time, and Proust, discovering a way to make time give back all it has taken, through turning life by way of the memory into art, left masterpieces that are like clocks themselves, giant clocks stationed for always out in the world, sounding for us the high hours of our literature. But from greatest to least, don't most novels reflect that personal subjective time that lived for their writers throughout the writing?

There is the constant evidence of it in a writer's tempo, harmony, the inflections of his work, the symmetry and proportions of the parts in the whole; in the felt rhythms of his prose, his emotion is given its truest and most spontaneous voice; the cadence which is his alone tells us—it would almost do so in spite of him—his belief or disbelief in the story he intends us to hear. But I have in mind something more than this governing of a writer's style.

Faulkner has spoken for the record of his difficulties in writing *The Sound and the Fury*, the novel he loved best and considered his most imperfect; he spoke of its four parts as four attempts, and four failures, to tell his story. In their own degree, many other novels give evidence in themselves of what this difficulty suggests: the novel's duration is in part the measurable amount of time the novelist needs to apprehend and harness what is before him; time is part of the writing too. The novel finished and standing free of him is not the mirror-reflection of that writing-time, but is its equivalent. A novel's duration is, in some respect, exactly how long it takes the particular author of a particular novel to explore its emotional resources, and to give his full powers to learning their scope and meeting their demands, and finding out their truest procedure.

In the very imperfections of *The Sound and the Fury*, which come of a giant effort pushed to its limit and still trying, lies a strength we may set above perfection. They are the human quotient, and honorable as the marks left by the hand-held chisel in bringing the figure out of recalcitrant stone—which is another way of looking at time.

Review of Selected Letters
of William Faulkner
[*1977*]

Eudora Welty reviewed Selected Letters of William Faulkner, *edited by Joseph Blotner, in the* New York Times Book Review *on February 6, 1977, pp. 1, 18–30. The version below is an expansion of the review published in the* Times.

WILLIAM FAULKNER'S wife and daughter had said he "would not have wanted such a volume. His personal letters were never remotely intended for publication," and Faulkner himself had written (to Malcolm Cowley): "I dont like having my private life and affairs available to just any and everyone who has the price of the vehicle it's printed in." Thus Joseph Blotner writes in his introduction to this volume. "So a book of selected Faulkner letters was a logical next step."

The logic has shifted from Faulkner's to his biographer Blotner's, but while I suppose we can have little doubt that this fierce guardian of his own privacy would have abominated the publication of his letters, we can doubt, too, that he would have been much surprised at its being done anyway. Publishing personal letters of a genius gone to his grave is a human act of man. And plainly, in Blotner's case, even a reverent act.

Therefore it is good to have the book done by an editor and a publisher who cared about Faulkner the man as well as Faulkner the artist. It's been assembled and edited with taste, the responsible, devoted and thorough job we would expect after the 1974 biography.

Jill Faulkner Summers gave Blotner access and permission to publish letters in her possession, a number of which he'd drawn upon or already published in the biography. Some recipients of letters withheld theirs, in whole or in part. Mr. Blotner doesn't say what proportion of the existing body of letters this absence represents, or name any of their recipients, if indeed he knows all these facts himself. In the letters published, a row of dots indicates where something is omitted, though without a clue as to how much—a sentence or half the letter; we aren't told whether it was the recipient or the editor who has cut it. (Blotner says he has excised some things.) "The editor and biographer must take what he can get," he says.

The letters are in chronological order, but not numbered, and not bracketed in any way; there is no sectioning by period of time of life or place—it's Oxford to New Orleans to Paris, Hollywood, New York, Stockholm, Egypt, Virginia and all the rest, and home again, from page 3 to page 465, all without an extra one-line space between. (There are brief explanatory notes to introduce some of the correspondents, and a good index, which will help you to find your place.) If this plan lacks something in imagination, still it is uninterfering.

Faulkner's letters are not "literary"; but they are very much letters about writing. They are the letters of a man living in the midst of his own world and his own society and kin, a man who was ardently and all by himself trying to do the thing he most passionately wanted to do, and by necessity earn the family living by it. The greatest number of the letters we have are those to his publishers and agents. "Yours to hand," he customarily begins them. Intimacy was no part of them; they were factual business letters, as telegraphic as an SOS, which they often were. We cannot miss the sound of desperation so often underneath: these were letters of life-and-death, about the wherewithal to survive, to keep alive his genius; he was so pressed that often he sent them off without signing them.

In 1932 he writes to his agent Ben Wasson: "I hope to hell Paramount takes Sanctuary. Dad left Mother solvent for only about a year. Then it is me."

In 1934 he is working on two novels, and writing one short story each month, trying to sell to the *Post*. "As I explained to you before," he writes Harrison Smith, "I have my own taxes and my mother's, and the possibility that Estelle's people will call on me before Feb. 1 and also my mother's and Dean's support, and occasional demands from my other two brothers which I can never anticipate . . . Then in March I have . . . insurance and income tax."

He writes agent Morton Goldman in 1935: "The man who said that the pinch of necessity, butchers and grocers bills and insurance hanging over his head, is good for an artist, is a damned fool."

From the start, Faulkner could look at his work, and thought an artist ought to, with the objectivity of (as he liked to say) a carpenter who'd built a henhouse. What he *thought* and *felt*, had worked in anguish to convey, must make its appearance in the work itself—it was the hen in the henhouse. But he had to look at all he wrote with recognition of its earning possibilities. "By God I've got to."

He steps up his pace to two short stories a week—"I dont know how long I can keep it up"—and still prophesies that his insurance premiums "will be difficult to meet and perhaps even impossible, unless I should produce a book which the movies would want—which God Himself could not promise Himself to write."

Through all this, when a publisher's comprehension of his problems was so vital, Faulkner's editors at Random House met his letters with unfaltering willingness to advance him money against the future. Faulkner appreciated his luck, which brought him in the course of time to Harrison Smith, Robert K. Haas, Saxe Commins, Bennett Cerf and Albert Erskine. In Hollywood, where he'd gone to buy himself time, he wrote to Harold Ober: "If they [Warner's] had any judgment of people, they would have realized before now that they would get a damn sight more out of me by throwing away any damned written belly-clutching contract and let us work together on simple good faith and decency, like with you and Random House." Ober, it ought to be said, must have been the most understanding of agents, as well as the most patient.

By 1940 Faulkner writes: "But maybe a man worrying about money can't write anything worth buying." To Haas he says: "I had planned, after finishing THE HAMLET, to try to earn enough from short stories by July 1 to carry me through the year, allow me six months to write another novel. I wrote six . . . the sort of pot boilers which the Post pays me $1,000.00 each for, because the best I could hope for good stories is 3 or 4 hundred . . . but only one of them has sold yet. Now I have not only wasted the mental effort and concentration which went into the trash, but the six months . . . as well as the time since March 15 which I have spent mortgaging my mares and colts one at a time to pay food and electricity and washing and such, and watching each mail train in hopes of a check. Now I have about run out of mules to mortgage."

Then he replies to Harold Ober in 1941 that no, he has no carbon of the story he'd sent. It was a story rewritten from a chapter of a novel under way and sent "first draft and in haste because I need money badly . . . In hopes that Post will take it and I can get a check next week, I am trying to make the revision desired from memory, without waiting to get back your copy. If it does not fit, please return your copy, and the revision by AIR MAIL and I will get it back the same day. Please sell it for something as soon as you can. I am in a situation where I will take almost anything for it or almost anything else I have or can write."

The *Post* found the rewrite acceptable and the story appeared in May, 1942. It was "The Bear."

But threats of oblivion were only increasing, and it was during the course of his being rescued from it that Faulkner put down the best things he ever said about his writing in a series of letters to Malcolm Cowley. The correspondence between the two men, later good friends, who had then never met, began in 1944 when Cowley put to Faulkner his idea of a Viking Portable Faulkner, to be compiled and edited by him. The story, like all Faulkner's life, is well known by now, but it remains suspenseful. We know that had it not been for the reemergence of Faulkner's work in the triumphant organization Cowley made of it for this volume, and Cowley's fresh literary insight, which called forth Faulkner's composition of the Compson genealogy called "Appendix/Compson 1699–1945," all Faulkner's work, already out of print then, might be worse than only out of print now—it might be half forgotten.

"I would like the piece," Faulkner initially replies to Cowley, "except the biography part. You are welcome to it privately, of course. But I think that if what one has thought and hoped and endeavored and failed at is not enough, if it must be explained and excused by what he had experienced, done or suffered, while he was not being an artist, then he and the one making the evaluation have both failed."

Then to the letter that's the masterpiece: "I'm trying primarily to tell a story, in the most effective way I can think of, the most moving, the most exhaustive. But I think even that is incidental to what I am trying to do . . . I am telling the same story over and over, which is myself and the world . . .

67

I am trying to go a step further [than Thomas Wolfe] . . . I'm trying to say it all in one sentence, between one Cap and one period. I'm still trying to put it all, if possible, on one pinhead. I don't know how to do it. All I know to do is to keep on trying in a new way . . . Life is a phenomenon but not a novelty . . . Art is simpler than people think because there is so little to write about. All the moving things are eternal in man's history and have been written before, and if a man writes hard enough, sincerely enough, humbly enough, and with the unalterable determination never never never to be quite satisfied with it, he will repeat them, because art like poverty takes care of its own, shares its bread."

On April 23, 1946, he has the book: "Dear Cowley: The job is splendid. Damn you to hell anyway. But even if I had beat you to the idea, mine wouldn't have been this good. By God, I didn't know myself what I had tried to do, and how much I had succeeded."

We have to fillet this story from where it lies embedded in the chronological pages, spread over a section fifty-one pages long. It's alongside letters like the kind one to Miss Lida, his mother-in-law, about the flowers in California, their likeness to and difference from the flowers in Mississippi, just because it comes next—telling us something about Faulkner's character and manners but holding us up when we want the next letter to Cowley. The letters, the best in Blotner's book, can still better be read in Cowley's own 1966 *Faulkner-Cowley File*, where they appear, along with the other side of the correspondence, in uninterrupted sequence, and where, so read, they can move you to tears.

But there are values in the chronological order of a special kind. When you read the letters above, embodying all Faulkner has taught himself about what he's doing, you can remember those he wrote back in 1925, when he walked over France in the greatest exuberance, planning to make his reputation abroad. He writes to his mother: "I have just written such a beautiful thing that I am about to bust—2000 words about the Luxembourg gardens and death."

The letters make us variously aware of Faulkner's Oxford, so often their background. A letter dated December 31,1948, to the president of the American Academy of Arts and Letters, which had been trying in vain to let Faulkner know he had been elected a member on November 23, explains it perfectly: "The letter must have become mislaid after it reached my home, since I did not receive it. I was in a deer hunting camp on Nov. 23. Telegrams are a casual business here; the office in town telephones them out and if you are not there to answer the phone, nothing else is done about it unless the operator happens to meet or pass you in the street and happens to remember to tell you a telegram came for you two or three weeks ago, did you get it?"

To Malcolm Cowley he remarks: "My whole town spent much of its time trying to decide just what living men I was writing about, the one literary criticism of the town being 'How in the hell did he remember all that, and when did that happen anyway?'"

And to Phil Mullen, of the Oxford *Eagle*, after the Nobel Prize award: "I fear that some of my fellow Mississippians will never forgive that 30,000$ that durn foreign country gave me for just sitting on my ass and writing stuff that makes my own state ashamed to own me."

But away from it, in Hollywood, he writes to A P. Hudson: "I dont like this damn place any better than I ever did. That is one comfort, at least I cant be any sicker tomorrow for Mississippi than I was yesterday."

It was all the same emotion, and what it was, the books made us know.

I have reported mostly on those letters that have to do with Faulkner's writing because Mr. Blotner says in his introduction that "The main purpose of this collection is to provide a deeper understanding of the artist, to reveal as much as possible what one can see in the letters about his art—its sources, intentions, the process of creation . . ." and also because I believe concentrating on letters about his work to be truest to Faulkner. Those letters that directly speak of his work are marvelous, and so are others that do so obliquely. All make clear that it remained the gift—not its cost in the work or its anguish, but the gift he had—that came first with him.

He writes to Joan Williams in 1953: ". . . And now, at last, I have some perspective on all I have done. I mean, the work apart from me, the work which I did, apart from what I am . . . And now I realize for the first time what an amazing gift I had: uneducated in every formal sense, without even very literate, let alone literary, companions, yet to have made the things I made. I dont know where it came from. I dont know why God or gods, or whoever it was, selected me to be the vessel. Believe me, this is not humility, false modesty: it is simply amazement."

Neither was it self-centered. Faulkner's marked sensitivity to others, to their pain, their needs of affection, encouragement, moral support, might have been taken for granted from the evidence of his work. What might not have been so easily guessed was that their gifts as artists brought about a profound response in him.

In the occasional—even rare—letter to a literary peer, his feeling for, appreciation of, the other writer's gift—not shoptalk—is almost sure to be the subject. Just as it is to a young unknown black poet whose manuscripts Faulkner read and helped him with: "Put the passion in it, but sit on the passion. Dont try to say to the reader what you want to say, but make him say it to himself *for* you. I will edit the second one and send it to you when I get it right . . . Your idea in both is all right." ("All right" emerges in Faulkner's letters as his strongest, surest term of praise.) He apparently fell in love with

Joan Williams, but the very touching letters to her all carry the current of a continuing wish to encourage her talent—she was in her twenties, just beginning to try to break away from the constrictions of family and write. He gave her his handwritten manuscript of *The Sound and the Fury*—a different sort of present from a bunch of roses.

Faulkner's letters show honesty, fairness and largeness of mind, genuine consideration for others, and compassion; also exhilaration and also despair. They pull no punches. They are in turn funny, sad, angry, desperate, tender, telegraphic, playful, quick in arithmetic and perfect in courtesy, unhappy. But these qualities, in one combination or another, and in some measure, can be found in the letters of a lot of human beings who didn't write *The Sound and the Fury*, "Spotted Horses," "The Bear." It would deny the author's whole intent, in a life-time of work and passion and stubborn, hellbent persistence, to look in his letters for the deepest revelations he made.

No man ever put more of his heart and soul into the written word than did William Faulkner. If you want to know all you can about that heart and soul, the fiction where he put it is still right there. The writer offered it to us from the start, and when we didn't even want it or know how to take it and understand it; it's been there all along and is more than likely to remain. Read that.

Speech in Celebration of the William Faulkner Postal Stamp [1987]

At the University of Mississippi on August 3, 1987, Eudora Welty joined Faulkner's daughter Jill Faulkner Summers, the literary critic Cleanth Brooks, and other dignitaries for the First Day of Issue ceremony of the William Faulkner stamp by U.S. Postal Service.

"I'm thrilled with being counted part of this group today," she said, "and thrilled with having lived in the same time as our great man we're honoring today."

LET US IMAGINE that here and now we're all in the old University Post Office and living in the twenties. We've come up to the stamp window to buy a 2-cent stamp, but we see nobody there. We knock and then we pound, and we pound again and there's not a sound back there. So we holler his name, and at last here he is. William Faulkner. We have interrupted him. Postmaster Faulkner's treatment of the mail could be described as offhand, with a strong local tradition and some soul who still can personally remember that during post office hours when he should have been putting up the mail and selling stamps at the window up front, he was out of sight in the back—writing lyric poems. He was a postmaster who made it hard for you in general to buy a stamp and send a letter or to get your hands on any of that mail that might have come to you. Faulkner the Postmaster called it quits

72

Eudora Welty with Jill Faulkner Summers, Faulkner's daughter,
at the unveiling of the William Faulkner postage stamp, University of Mississippi, 1987

here in 1924. Faulkner the Poet was able to move on with his pen into his vast prose world of Yoknapatawpha County.

So here we are today, and it might have tickled the future great master of comedy if he could know that the real tale of his post office career came to its close not in 1924 but today. Sixty-three years later the tale ends with a postage stamp. The occasion is the issue of a stamp named in his honor with his portrait on it. It's as if the United States Postal Service had forgiven him for the mail he had lost in the trash barrel in the light of his proven deserts in other fields, beginning with what he was doing there in the back room.

Once portraits of our presidents of the United States seemed obligatory to make postage stamps the real authentic thing. It took George Washington or Thomas Jefferson in the upper right-hand corner of your letter to make the letter go. But a more imaginative tradition has happily grown up in the designing of our postage stamps today. William Faulkner will be in good literary company—T. S. Eliot, Emily Dickinson, Nathaniel Hawthorne, Herman Melville, Willa Cather, Edith Wharton.

Of course here in Oxford and at the Faulkner conference going on at the University, we keep hearing people asking one another, "What would *Faulkner* have thought of the Faulkner stamp?" If the man himself were here, and available for questioning, he would be asked the inevitable question of our times: "Mr. Faulkner, sir, how do you *feel* about having a stamp named in your honor?"

Well, who knows what the great man might have said? He might have suggested that the portrait painted by his mother might have possibly improved it. He might simply have observed that stamps have gone up since he had anything to do with the postal system, from 2 cents to 22. Again, he might have just gone on puffing at his pipe, meditating, as we see him on the stamp. My only guess today is that William Faulkner would have accepted his stamp because he knew what an honor was.

For all of us—scholars, teachers, writers, and collectors brought here today for the value of the rarity of the stamp itself—it's unavoidable that we should be reminded of a key statement Faulkner once came to write: "I discovered my own little postage stamp of native soil was worth writing about and that I would never live long enough to exhaust it and that by sublimating the actual into the apocryphal, I would have complete liberty to use whatever talent I might have to its absolute top." As we celebrate the first day of issue of the William Faulkner stamp, we do so in this awareness that this writer remains himself a bringer of the written word, that he is himself that rare thing—the rarest—a genius. He exists, as he always did, in the world at large for anyone to whom the written word travels. The stamp can stand for that, too. It serves as a symbol of communication.

AFTERWORD: WELTY AND FAULKNER AND THE SOUTHERN LITERARY TRADITION

Noel Polk

The eye of William Faulkner is a defining eye. Generations of post-Faulkner Southern writers and readers have adopted his vision and so seen "the South" through his experience rather than through their own, or struggled against that vision, as a barrier to be gone through or over or around. In either case, Faulkner's vision has defined what can be seen, so that Southern writers following Faulkner are indeed in a double bind. But as large and encompassing as Faulkner's vision is, it is, finally, only a single vision, and he would have been less likely than anyone else to assume that his was the only one.

Discussions of the relationships between William Faulkner and Southern writers following him have been largely hamstrung because they are normally driven, willy-nilly, by questions of Faulkner's influence, questions with which interviewers have plagued writers who have had to operate in Faulkner's wake if not always in his shadow. Because the questions assume that the subsequent generations are both junior and inferior, these writers have spent far too much of their energy escaping and denying—*dealing with*—Faulkner's legacy, even if only in being conscious of reviewers' inevitable for-better-or-worse comparisons of their work with the tradition of "Southern" letters that Faulkner so forcefully defined.

Their denials, of course, are the most compelling evidence of how completely inescapable he and his work are. The interviews and the criticism would suggest that as a generation they engage in a collective fretting, wailing, like Quentin Compson at the end of *Absalom, Absalom!*: "I dont hate him! I dont! I dont! I dont hate him!" On the other hand, it may be that what they are really saying is not *I dont hate him* but rather, *I hate that question. I hate it. Why do professors keep asking me that question?* It must be difficult enough for writers to grapple honestly with Faulkner's Founding Presence in the tradition, without having to respond to interviewers' presumptive questions about an influence they may not completely understand, or need to care about, having books to write and better things to do.

In point of fact, then, probably more critics than writers have been overwhelmed by Faulkner, more critics than writers have felt that Faulkner alone has defined the terms by which we can talk about the South. Thus writers like Walker Percy and Barry Hannah, who deal with a more urban world than Faulkner does, a world more directly a part of their own experiences than Faulkner's, have occasionally had a hard time with many traditional critics, who believe that they therefore represent a decline in "Southern literature," whatever that is. As Thomas L. McHaney has suggested, the old guard of Southern critics want to penalize Southern writers who have indoor plumbing and give extra credit to them if they write about people who do not.[1] To my knowledge, Hannah has not addressed himself seriously to the problem (although he has done a bit of Welty-bashing, perhaps his own version of escaping "the influence"), but Percy, with more than a little wit, spent more time than he should have actually denying that he is a Southern writer, and Richard Ford has written that all writers, even Southerners, should be left alone to create their own categories of expectation.

But I seem already on the verge of defending Eudora Welty against some accusation or other.[2] This defensive posture seems inevitable under any circumstance that forces us to consider *Faulkner and* whoever, just as we Faulknerians somehow always seem to wind up defending him against charges of subordinance such as govern discussions of James Joyce and Faulkner or Shakespeare and Faulkner—which discussions are also nearly always driven by questions of influence or borrowing. It is as though critics must or do always operate chronologically, following T. S. Eliot's "Tradition and the Individual Talent" and, more recently, Harold Bloom's *Anxiety of Influence*, without recognizing that writers do not necessarily operate chronologically and that what they derive from their predecessors may not be anything that they can or need to articulate or that critics can possibly understand. And since Bloom deals exclusively with male writers and oedipal struggles with their predecessors, it is certainly worth noting that women writers stand in an entirely different relationship to the "tradition," and it would be surprising indeed if they dealt with it in the same way male writers do; we have fostered a good deal of misunderstanding of women writers, especially Southern women, by assuming that they do.

Eudora Welty, quite simply, has mostly had none of this question: she has not even generally entertained the question of Faulkner's influence on her as worth her time. "It was like living near a mountain," she says, with characteristic and modest acknowledgment of The Presence in north Mississippi. Unspoken in her image, and perhaps even unthought, is the simple fact that what most often lives near a mountain is another mountain.

It is fairly easy to trace the points at which Welty's and Faulkner's lives intersected. It was not often, even though they lived barely 150 miles apart. Faulkner wrote her from Hollywood in 1943: "Dear Welty," he wrote, "You are doing fine. You are doing all right." He then named *The Robber Bridegroom* and the "collection called GREEN something" and "The Gilded Six Bits"—a story by Zora Neale Hurston, which he had mistakenly thought was one of Welty's, perhaps because Zora and Eudora rhyme. He told her that he thought of Djuna Barnes when he read *The Robber Bridegroom* but expected her to pass that. He asked about her background, then confessed that he had not read Green something yet but "expect nothing from it because I expect from you. You are doing very fine. Is there any way I can help you? How old are you?"[3]

According to Welty, they met occasionally at Faulkner's home in Oxford, ate dinner, sang hymns, and went sailing, but never discussed writing or literature. She reviewed *Intruder in the Dust* in 1949[4] and responded to Edmund Wilson's *New Yorker* attack on *Intruder* with a savagely funny indictment of Wilson's condescending presumption that Faulkner's Southern *material*, rather than his intellect or even his hard work, was responsible for the quality of his work and that Faulkner would have been a better writer if he had spent more time in such literary centers as New York talking to such writers as Edmund Wilson about literature.[5] Welty's response to this pomposity was, I think, the germ of her thoughts about the relationship between a writer's geographical place and the quality of the writing, thoughts that resulted in her well-known (and much misunderstood and much abused) essay of six years later called "Place in Fiction."[6] She reviewed Joseph Blotner's edition of Faulkner's letters in 1977[7] and used examples from his work as illustrations in several essays, among them "Place in Fiction," "Some Notes on Time in Fiction,"[8] and *Short Stories*. Faulkner mentioned Welty once more, in the late 1950s, during his time at the University of Virginia where, when asked about Welty, he again mentioned *The Robber Bridegroom*. They met a couple of months before his death in New York, at a ceremony during which Welty presented him with the Gold Medal for Fiction of the National

Institute of Arts and Letters. She wrote an elegant obituary for the Associated Press upon his death in July 1962.

So far as I can determine, this is the sum total of their public interaction. Privately, of course, we have no way of knowing what, if anything, they meant to each other. There is no evidence that Faulkner borrowed anything from Welty, and, for all of her manifest reverence for his work, for all that she claimed to have learned from him, there is no more evidence that she ever borrowed a single line or character or scene from him or ever crossed the state line of his Mississippi except as a grateful reader. Perhaps she made some conscious effort to honor the claim he had staked and simply avoided his territory. More likely, she saw a different landscape than the one he saw and so had no need to mine his. But her work does respond to his in significant ways that suggest that in her manifest reverence she was by no means unaware of his sources in a problematic tradition or uncritical of the implications of his accomplishment for those standing in a different relation to that tradition.

It is no credit to the scholarly world that Welty and Faulkner have been lumped together by traditionalist critics who have wanted to see them as somehow both empowered and limited by their "place" in Mississippi, who have argued that their literary strengths lie directly in their roots in the South (instead of in their brains), and who therefore, for example, have found it necessary (or convenient) to dismiss the relatively few works that they had the temerity to set outside Mississippi, as though they had committed gratuitous acts of literary suicide. Welty, of course, has suffered most in traditionalist readings of her work. Even sympathetic and admiring critics have seen her fiction as a sort of genteel, domestic, nonaggressive, *female* version of Faulkner and, to paraphrase her comment about Faulkner, we have generally asked her to stand on a lower step when posing for the group photograph.[9]

Faulkner's work self-consciously addresses epic issues and deals with them on an epic scale, in an epic landscape: his language strains at its own outermost limits to raise every event, every gesture, to its highest, most intense pitch of significance. The universe is his world; he moves fluidly and freely within it, and he strides with the certainty of a colossus to get where he wants to go. His novels deliberately engage the "great" themes of Western literature, and his tragedies and comedies are rich in their analyses of culture and of human life in the twentieth century. The problems with this reading of Faulkner (as of other canonical male writers), as we have finally begun to learn from feminist critics, are the operating assumptions behind traditionalist views, which hold as given that Faulkner's historically canonized themes and epic struggles are larger, more cosmic, more significantly responsive to crises in Western culture and so are therefore more important than the seemingly tamer, less grandiose, more domestic work of Welty—and other women writers, of course.

Driven by these assumptions of what constitutes "great" literature, traditionalist critics have paid the wrong kind of attention to the surface geniality—the face of the familiar—of much of Welty's fiction and have missed how profoundly, how troublingly, she has opened up the atom of the domestic and found there another universe, her own, an infinity of space that affords her an absolutely original engagement with the world and, more particularly, with the Western and Southern literary tradition that both defined and delimited her, though hardly in the ways we have assumed.[10] She slices away at the exteriors of the familiar, a familiar that is Southern only incidentally, and takes us into the hardest to reach nooks and crannies of human life. She dissects our comfortable assumptions about family, about community, about ourselves, and in doing so she offers us a more comprehensive, a more intensely local, understanding of those traditionally cosmic concerns than Faulkner does, precisely because she demonstrates how these "cosmic" concerns work on us, individually, in the most private, the least dramatic, least epical, places of our lives.

Welty thus offers alternative visions of our relationship with the cosmos, equally powerful visions that suggest other, equally potent options for responding to our worlds, options that may threaten us in ways that Faulkner's traditional vision does not. His world is tragic; things fall apart: we live, we suffer, we die. But in Faulkner we usually know who the enemy is, what the stakes are, we know that we must struggle, and we know how to struggle. In spite of her vision of the universe's wholeness, however, Welty's world is considerably harder to negotiate than Faulkner's, precisely because she knows that the enemy is not so easily recognizable, that the battleground is more nearly the minefield of our own backyards than the "universe." For her, and for her readers, the enemy is terrifyingly close; it resides permanently in and is inextricable from those structures of family and community that traditional readings of Southern literature always invoke as the enduring source of value in Southern life.

One of Faulkner's most touching pieces is the quasi-autobiographical "Mississippi," which he published in 1953 at a time when he had just begun an overtly political engagement with his native state, writing letters to editors and essays and giving speeches in which he argued against the racial status quo.[11] "Mississippi" is an eloquent and moving record of his attempts to grapple with the problems and pressures his native land had caused for him and of his reconciliation with past and present Mississippi.

The protagonist of "Mississippi" is Faulkner the citizen, not Faulkner the artist. He makes this distinction clear throughout by referring to the citizen in the third person—"he," "the boy," "the young man," "the man," "the mid-dleaged," "the gray-haired"—and by refusing to speak of his career as a writer, although we are never very far from that career: "Mississippi"'s narrative moves freely, fluidly, back and forth between Faulkner's two Mississippis, as if to demonstrate just how thin the line separating them is.

"Mississippi"'s opening pages outline the state's history from its beginnings in "the alluvial swamps"(11), bring it up through the prehistoric Indian inhabitants, the European settlers, the frontier, the cotton economy, the Civil War, Emancipation, Reconstruction, and right on up to the end of the nineteenth century, when "the boy" is born into that powerful flood of specifically Southern history. Though he will be a child of the twentieth century, the forces shaping his life as a Mississippian are very much those of the nineteenth: the boy hears about the Civil War even before he hears about Santa Claus at Christmas, and the first character he speaks of from his childhood is Mammy Callie, the family nurse, a former slave who refused to leave the Faulkners after Emancipation and who was to survive into Faulkner's forty-third year, a constant reminder that the Civil War and Reconstruction in the South are not mere historical circumstances but ever-present, daily realities. She plays a little game with the family, constantly reminding them that they "owe" her $89 in back wages, wages—the dollars, at any rate—that have been offered over and over again and which she has refused to accept (16). This "debt" becomes Faulkner's gentle, unforced metaphor for all that white Mississippi owes to its black citizens, that it will never repay partly because Mammy Callie—the Negro—does not really want the debt wiped out and partly because what is owed cannot really be repaid. Along with the chief protagonist, Mammy Callie is "Mississippi"'s most important character. Her life runs through the essay as a moving counterpoint to the boy's own maturation.

She sees the child into his life; "Mississippi" reaches its elegiac end as "the middleaging" sees her out of hers, delivering her funeral oration and "hoping that when his turn came there would be someone in the world to owe him the sermon which all owed to her who had been, as he had been from infancy, within the scope and range of that fidelity and that devotion and that rectitude" (42). Her death is the thematic climax of "Mississippi," and in her life and death are encapsulated all that Faulkner's citizen protagonist has learned in his progression from infancy to middle age about his native state: how, that is, one can be so completely a victim—of color, of law, of economics—as Mammy Callie had been and still find room to love even that which had victimized her; and how it might be possible for him, the middleaging, both to hate the people and the system that had victimized Mammy Callie and to follow her example in being able to find something to love, even in her oppressors.

"Mississippi" moves to closure as "the man" returns from travel to find himself "Home again, his native land; he was born of it and his bones will sleep in it" (36). His first articulation of an emotional reconciliation with Mississippi recognizes that love and hate are not mutually exclusive: "loving it even while hating some of it" (36). He hates the greed, he writes, the waste of the lumbermen and the land speculators who changed the face of the landscape by cutting down the big trees for timber, moving the Big Woods farther and farther away from the areas he hunted in as a child. "But most of all," he writes,

> he hated the intolerance and injustice: the lynching of Negroes not for the crimes they committed but because their skins were black . . .; the inequality: the poor schools they had then when they had any, the hovels they had to live in unless they wanted to live outdoors: who could worship the white man's God but not in the

white man's church; pay taxes in the white man's courthouse but couldn't vote in it or for it; working by the white man's clock but having to take his pay by the white man's counting . . . ; the bigotry which could send to Washington some of the senators and congressmen we sent there and which could erect in a town no bigger than Jefferson five separate denominations of churches but set aside not one square foot of ground where children could play and old people could sit and watch them. (37–38)

"Mississippi" concludes with Mammy Callie's death, the gathering of her children, her laying out, and the middleaging's funeral sermon, all of which build to the essay's final paragraph, Faulkner's second, more complex articulation of the relationship between love and hate: "Loving all of it even while he had to hate some of it because he knows now that you dont love because: you love despite; not for the virtues, but despite the faults" (42–43).

For Faulkner, as I say, the struggle is always epic, a heroic confrontation between contending forces—love and hate; justice and injustice; life and death—that are eternally antagonistic to each other and to human peace: one lives only under the terms of existential combat. It is an intensely moral struggle, with Faulkner, humanity—*man* he would say—caught in the middle of an irresolvable universal conflict whose antagonisms are permanently fixed in the nature of things. In Faulkner the best we can hope is to turn the tension itself into part of our weaponry, to counter force not with reason but with superior force: you don't love *because,* you love *despite*; you choose what you will struggle for and against, and you wrestle to the ground those opposing forces that would have you doubt the meaning or validity of your choices. For Faulkner, then, it is a matter of will, of main strength, a test of himself against the cosmos.

There is in all this, of course, a tragic heroism, attractive and indeed essential to those of us raised in his tradition. But the Pyrrhic irony of Faulkner's victory—*our* victory, too, when we manage it—is that to assert victory is simultaneously to admit defeat: to win he must submit to the *ought*, the *should*, the moral imperatives that require him to love despite when he can't find a sufficient because, imperatives that derive from the value systems of the cultural tradition of which he is so vital a part. The victory thus requires him to suppress his own powerful emotions of despair and frustration in favor of the communal mandate that love is better than hate, reconciliation better than alienation.

Put so baldly, of course, these sentiments are hard to argue with. Who wouldn't prefer the comforts of love and community to wandering alone in the existential wasteland of the twentieth century? At the same time, their baldness permits us to see them also as platitudes, which like all platitudes operate in the service of a cultural status quo, offering themselves up as Truth that ratifies and ensures a community's cohesion and stability. But such platitudes, uncritically enforced, take communities one step beyond stability and into rigidity. Faulkner's powerful conclusions in "Mississippi," of course, beg numerous questions that his fiction does not; indeed, most of his fiction offers very precise analyses of the dangers of cultural stasis. But even the fiction, finally, in its assumptions, or perhaps assertions, of its own universality, also begs many of the same questions about the hierarchical structures of community and about their profoundly different effects on men and women. In "Mississippi" and elsewhere, Faulkner takes for granted his own capacity—indeed, his need, often articulated as an artistic credo: life is motion, stasis is death—always to keep in motion, to avoid the rigidity that his platitudes here clearly can lead to. As a male, Faulkner bears a different relationship to the tradition that valorizes "love" and "reconciliation," that prefers its own definitions of "justice" and "injustice," "family" and "community," than women do. As a man, like Welty's King MacLain, Faulkner can choose what he wants to love and be reconciled with. Women traditionally do not have that freedom: to them falls the dailiness of love and reconciliation, of cohesion, their practice rather than their rhetorizing. Thus it seems not only fair but necessary to ask just *how* and *why* love is better than hate, reconciliation better than alienation: for whom are they better?

These are, I think, important questions in Welty's *The Golden Apples* and central to that collection's magnificent final story, "The Wanderers," which, like "Mississippi," also involves a homecoming, a confrontation with these same contending emotions of love and hate, the same challenge of reconciliation. Her responses to them are quite different from Faulkner's. Virgie Rainey, the chief character of "The Wanderers," is "over 40" years old. Like King MacLain, the heroic and fascinating wanderer of the town's romanticizing imagination, she too has been away from Morgana, for her own reasons and we do not know where, and has some time before now come home. She is a subdued version of her "June Recital" self, the wild and free spirit who as an adolescent rejected the tyranny of Miss Eckhart's metronome; she is obliged now in her middle age to care for a senile and problematic mother, who forces her to submit to the deadening metronomic regularity of domestic life in Morgana, of which Miss Eckhart's hated metronome is the collection's metaphor.

Welty's staging of the ritualized activities of Virgie's mother's funeral—the coming and going, the visits, the laying out of the body, the gestures of sympathy, Virgie's necessary (and unwelcome) commingling with all these figures from her life (none of whom, she notes, except Snowdie MacLain, has ever been to visit her or her mother)—is Welty's unrelentingly unsentimental and often savagely funny analysis of such communal rituals. The story's spine is Virgie's growing capacity to admit to herself just how and why she is different from, and also just how little she cares for or needs, any of these folks whom Faulkner's tradition would ask her to love despite; how little she cares for this "community," nominally and traditionally the center of value in Southern life. In fact, Virgie discovers a wonderfully liberating and purifying capacity to hate, to be angry, which becomes her salvation precisely because it frees her from the need to love or even tolerate any of them, her own mother included, much less to continue to live among them.

Several times throughout the day of the funeral she deliberately shuns all contact—"Don't touch me," she repeats to Cassie and others, who touch her in embrace or pull her in one direction or another and who ignore her demands to be left alone. Virgie's efforts to be physically separate from them reaches a moment of high comedy in one of the closing scenes in which Cassie—who wants desperately to force Virgie to feel about her mother as she, Cassie, is obligated to feel about her own mother, a suicide—chases Virgie out of town in her car, pulls up beside her, and drives side by side out of town with her; they shout at each other through the open windows, Cassie forcing a conversation that Virgie clearly doesn't want to have; Cassie insists that Virgie drive by her yard to see how she has spelled out her own mother's name in 232 narcissus bulbs, to ensure her return every spring.

Most of all Virgie wants to be free of her mother. One of the story's most affecting scenes culminates in the moment of Katie's death, as Virgie fans her: "The clock jangled faintly as cymbals struck under water, but did not strike; it couldn't." There is no Faulknerian dingdong of Time and Doom here but rather a liberating pulse of time now become accommodating and friendly. The clock jangles "faintly," not in alarm but as a sign of some impending revelation, something just about to be understood; the "cymbals struck under water" (431)[12] likewise suggest some stirring impulse of fanfare, of celebration, of simple unadmittable delight in her freedom that she is not, at this moment, prepared to let become conscious but which will provide the specific energy for her reactions through the rest of the story. She realizes, at the moment of her mother's death, that she herself is "not much afraid of death, either of its delay or its surprise" (431), and she feels "a torrent of riches . . . flow over the room, submerging it, loading it with what was over-sweet" (432). Not her years of self-sacrifice but her mother's long overdue death offers her release from the prison of home and family and community that her self-sacrifice has placed her in.

She endures the opening skirmishes with the visitors who come when they hear that Katie is dead. When in the evening they leave, they seem in their parting "to drag some mythical gates and barriers away from her view" (439) making it possible for her to see what she has never been able to see: the world "shimmers" in the "lighted distance" when she sees the "little last crescent of hills before the country of the river, and the fields" (439). In the face of human death, the cotton fields still "look busy on Sunday; even while they are not being picked they push out their bloom the same" (439). She sees, for the first time, a landscape artificially divided into families and property and seasons and even meteorological conditions: "the frail screens of standing trees still measured, broke, divided—Stark from Loomis from Spights from Holifield, and the summer from the rain" (439). Welty punctuates Virgie's meditations on these divisions with the appearance of Old Plez's ancient automobile, which appears to Virgie "cracked like some put-together puzzle of the globe of the world. Its cracks didn't meet from one side across to the other, and was all held together with straightened-out baling wire, for today" (439). Like Plez's car, Morgana is a ramshackle vehicle, held together by no more force than the used baling wire of tradition.

Her mother having gone to the underworld, this Virgie/Virgo/Persephone releases herself to the upper world, not in the spring for the plowing and the harvest but in the fall—September, the month of Virgo—the time of harvest. She has reached her own fullness: at more than forty Virgie is at least premenopausal, and so free, or nearly, not just of her own history (now that her mother is dead) but even of the metronomic cycles of her own body that have bound her to time, to the rhythms of the earth, even to the natural rhythms of life and death. In a quite extraordinary passage, Virgie goes down to the river for a swim:

It was bright as mid-afternoon in the openness of the water, quiet and peaceful. She took off her clothes and let herself into the river.

She saw her waist disappear into reflectionless water; it was like walking into sky, some impurity of skies. All was one warmth, air, water, and her own body. All seemed one weight, one matter—until as she put down her head and closed her eyes and the light slipped under her lids, she felt this matter a translucent one, the river, herself, the sky all vessels which the sun filled. She began to swim in the river, forcing it gently, as she would wish for gentleness to her body. Her breasts around which she felt the water curving were as sensitive at that moment as the tips of wings must feel to birds, or antennae to insects. She felt the sand, grains intricate as little cogged wheels, minute shells of old seas, and the many dark ribbons of grass and mud touch her and leave her, like suggestions and withdrawals of some bondage that might have been dear, now dismembering and losing itself. She moved but like a cloud in skies, aware but only of the nebulous edges of her feeling and the vanishing opacity of her will, the carelessness for the water of the river through which her body had already passed as well as for what was ahead. The bank was all one, where out of the faded September world the little ripening plums started. Memory dappled her like no more than a paler light, which in slight agitations came through leaves, not darkening her for more than an instant. The iron taste of the old river was sweet to her, though. If she opened her eyes she looked at blue-bottles, the skating waterbugs. If she trembled it was at the smoothness of a fish or snake that crossed her knees.

In the middle of the river, whose downstream or upstream could not be told by a current, she lay on her stretched arm, not breathing, floating. Virgie had reached the point where in the next moment she might turn into something without feeling it shock her. She hung suspended in the Big Black River as she would know to hang suspended in felicity. Far to the west, a cloud running fingerlike over the sun made her splash the water. She stood, walked along the soft mud of the bottom and pulled herself out of the water by a willow branch, which like warm rain brushed her back with its leaves.

At a distance, two little boys lying naked in the red light on the sandbar looked at her as she disappeared into the leaves. (439–40)

This is a remarkably Emersonian passage, and its resonances with Faulkner's "The Bear" seem also unmistakable and deliberate. But Virgie is no transparent eyeball, she is no Isaac McCaslin bemoaning the loss of the Big Woods. Far from contending with it or from seeing herself as in any way separate from it or even transparent in it, Virgie *becomes* the universe, the constellation Virgo; she melds with it, absorbs it, assumes her position in the larger, the truly "universal," scheme of things as unselfconsciously and magisterially as Botticelli's Venus.

This scene occurs early, hard on the heels of her mother's death. From this point Virgie gradually divests herself of all the impedimenta of her containment in Morgana—her childhood friends, the remnants of her father's family, who come only to funerals; her parents' generation, who have gossiped her into running away; the men she's worked for, slept with, including her sailor lover Kewpie Moffatt (whom she misremembers, with a puckish smile, as Bucky); Miss Eckhart and a countrywoman's dead baby, both of whom she remembers as she walks through the cemetery: and both of whom, she realizes and admits, she hates.

But free now to hate, she discovers that in fact she doesn't hate Miss Eckhart, and she understands that

she has never doubted that all the opposites on earth were close together, love close to hate, living to dying; but of them all, hope and despair were the closest blood—unrecognizable one from the other sometimes, making moments double upon themselves, and in the doubling double again, amending but never taking back. (452–530)

Almost simultaneously with this revelation, near the end of the story, Virgie sits majestically alone, contemplating all her possibilities. The earth and sky gather around her, stopping their motion, in salute and approbation:

It was ripe afternoon, and all about her was that light in which the earth seems to come into its own, as if there would be no more days, only this day—when fields glow like deep pools and the expanding trees at their edges seem almost to open, like lilies, golden or dark. She had always loved that time of day, but now, alone, untouched now, she felt like dancing; knowing herself not really, in her essence, yet hurt; and thus happy. The chorus of crickets was as unprogressing and out of time as the twinkling of a star. (453)

This is a paradigmatic moment in Welty, one she will repeat, with variations, in the stories of *The Bride of the Innisfallen*: a moment in which a lone woman comes to herself in a dark wood but responds to it not as a moment of fear and perplexity, but rather savors it as a moment of epiphany, in which she discovers that she can be happy alone and stops to luxuriate in her freedom.

In "Mississippi" Faulkner resolves his conflicts with his home, his place, by overcoming his hatred not with love so much as with the will to love, so that the exercise of love is an act of main strength that must subdue hate, suppress it as something inimical to love. Virgie, by contrast, overcomes the cultural mandate to love her family and friends by giving herself permission to hate them. She discovers that hatred is purgative and liberating in ways that love can never be: hate does not require the suppression of what you love, but love often tyrannically demands the suppression of the things you hate. The freedom to hate can bring us closer to the things we love because in the free exercise of both emotions we can come closer to our own true terribly complex selves: as Virgie comes to understand, hate and love, hope and despair, are not antagonists at all, as in Faulkner's vision, but closely connected, intimate, and essential to our human wholeness.

This is not a Eudora Welty that we are accustomed to or prepared to accept. We have preferred to think of her as a gentle purveyor of the domestic, the odd, the grotesque. We have been comfortable reading her through the critical language of Southern literary studies that developed about the time Welty began her publishing career. That language has never been large enough to contain either Faulkner or Welty, but it has worked most perniciously to keep us from understanding Welty. By reading her through such so-called Southern filters as place, humor, race, history, and the grotesque, our critical vocabulary, our cultural assumptions, have protected us from the parts of Welty's work that might unsettle and threaten us since they are actually subversive of those so-called values of family and community—place—that are so much a part of what we have been taught to think of as central to "Southern" literature.

But we can no longer ignore what is so manifestly *there* in Welty's work. In *The Golden Apples* she rewrites Southern literature, or at least provides us an opportunity to erase it and start over. The "community" of Morgana is a community only in the sense that a group of people live more or less together geographically. Mrs. Stark knows that one old woman owes another old woman a decent and respectable funeral, but nothing in the book suggests that anybody in this "community" feels any obligation to the living, to themselves or any other. Morgana, like the Southern communities of our agrarian traditions, worships the metronomic rhythms of night and day, of lunar and menstrual cycles and seasonal change. Instead of offering change and renewal, however, the natural rhythms of *The Golden Apples* become other forms of communal limitation, which Virgie and King MacLain have resisted but to which the community has prostrated itself because it cannot see beyond the next tick of the clock, the next five P.M. when the cows need calling and milking, the next spring when we must plant. As a "community," then, Morgana constantly turns inward, using its rituals of life, death, and June recitals, not to regenerate itself but merely to replicate. Morgana is thus trapped in the deadening circularity of cycles: it worships its seasons, its rituals, its monuments, its cemeteries: finally, it worships death. Perhaps death is the only way out of the cycle: suicide is not unknown in Morgana.

Through no particular act of her own, Virgie no longer has to submit to these rhythms. Free of her past, she no longer has to replicate her life from one day to the next; she can now regenerate a free and independent self, one yet to be discovered, or perhaps one that can be *re*covered from her "June Recital" adolescence. Looking outward, she exfoliates, enlarges, and *becomes* the universe with which Faulkner so constantly and epically contends and to which the people of Morgana have long since surrendered. At the story's close, true to her name, Virgie has brought rain to the wasteland and she sits under a tree. The French origins of her name suggest that she has become Virgie *reine*, Virgie the Queen, the Virgin Queen, Aphrodite and Virgo, sitting on a stile throne with her back to the MacLain courthouse—the house of the court, the royal palace of the king. As Danièle Pitavy-Souques has suggested, it could specifically be the Yoknapatawpha County courthouse to which Virgie and Welty have turned their backs.[13] It is certainly the symbolic counting house of the political landscape of the Southern literary tradition that Faulkner's courthouse so powerfully symbolizes. Her back squarely turned to that courthouse and that tradition, Virgie looks not inward but outward, facing the rich, lubricious, and delicious landscape of her own future: the landscape of possibility.

This, too, is a paradigmatic moment in Welty, a repetition of the earlier one when the universe stopped to acknowledge her freedom. It is a striking moment and difficult to understand because we are not accustomed to seeing women happy *and* alone, happy *because* alone. Likewise, and perhaps even more important, traditional readings of "Southern" literature teach us to believe that change is loss, that loss is a bad thing, that what we lose is always more valuable than what we gain: all this because change always involves a direct assault on the "old verities"—the *old* verities, verities *because* old, and always inextricable from our communal memories of a past that was somehow better, more stable, than the present. We have thus too easily accepted a "sense of place" as a mantra of Southern literary study and have been reluctant to understand how often history, or sense of the past, of place, keeps the present in a virtual chokehold. I hasten to point out that though many of Faulkner's characters and critics make the mistake of idealizing the past so strongly as to resist change, Faulkner himself never does. He constantly argues that the capacity to cope with change is the test of maturity in an individual; but even these terms—*cope* and *test*—testify to the intensity of the moral struggle that change entails for a people whose individual and communal lives, their places in time and space, are invested in the values of the past, those "old" verities.

In this struggle, Morgana is undoubtedly a Faulknerian, a Southern, community. This is precisely the community that Virgie, at the end of "The Wanderers," is poised to reject. She sees change not as loss but as opportunity, as possibility; if she chooses, she can now step aside from history, as so many of Faulkner's characters want desperately to do but cannot. Virgie refuses to be imprisoned in the past, and she faces a future limited only by the choices she is now, as never before, capable of making. She is willing to discover new verities, new configurations of social organization, that could give new and vital meaning to her life.

We are prepared to be thrilled and moved by the traditional visions of the William Faulkners. We are not so prepared to be discomfited and challenged by "the wildness of the world behind the woman's view." But that view, especially Eudora Welty's, can give us a fix on the most intimate and frightening parts of our lives that the Faulkners, with all their clashing and clanging and self-conscious commitment to Cosmic Significance, never have. Faulkner of course saw what he saw, as Shakespeare did, and we are immeasurably the richer for it. But he didn't see it all, nobody can, and like Shakespeare he saw what his tradition allowed him to see.

Eudora Welty's eye, too, is a defining eye, but it is also a subversive eye that looks at things other eyes don't know to look at or, worse, avoid. But hers too can be an enlarging and enriching vision if we have the courage to see what she is showing us instead of what we want to see.

1. Thomas L. McHaney, Review of Walter Sullivan, *A Requiem for the Renaissance. Mississippi Quarterly* 30 (1976–77): 185–88.

2. The portions of this essay on Welty are adapted from my "The Landscape of Illusion in Eudora Welty's 'The Wanderers,'" in *Southern Landscape*, ed. Tony Badger, Walter Edgar, and Jan Nordby Gretland (Tübingen: Stauffenburg-Verlag, 1996), 236–42.

3. Joan St. C. Crane, "William Faulkner to Eudora Welty: A Letter," *Mississippi Quarterly* 42 (1989): 223–28.

4. Eudora Welty, *The Eye of the Story* (New York: Random House, 1979), 207–11.

5. Eudora Welty, "Department of Amplification," *New Yorker* 24 (January 1, 1949): 41–42.

6. Welty, *Eye of the Story*, 116–33.

7. Ibid., 212–20.

8. Ibid., 163–73.

9. Welty, "Department of Amplification," 41–42.

10. See, for example, Rebecca Mark, *The Dragon's Blood: Feminist Intertextuality in Eudora Welty's "The Golden Apples"* (Jackson, University Press of Mississippi, 1994).

11. All references to "Mississippi" are to the edition by James B. Meriwether in *Essays, Speeches, and Public Letters by William Faulkner* (New York: Random House, 1965); page numbers are noted parenthetically in the text.

12. All references to "The Wanderers" are to Welty's *Collected Stories* (New York: Harcourt Brace Jovanovich, 1980) and are noted parenthetically in the text.

13. Danièle Pitavy-Souques, *La Mort de Méduse* (Lyon: Presses Universitaires de Lyon, 1992), 47.